ideals
Scrap Book

editor
van b. hooper

This new IDEALS SCRAPBOOK has been specially prepared to acquaint our new friends with the type and quality of inspiring poetry, prose, photographs, art, and full color reproductions that are featured in EVERY issue of IDEALS.

These are typical pages — selected at random from previous volumes of IDEALS.

Each issue of IDEALS features one principal theme — some of the subjects have included Christmas — Mothers — Historic — Friendly — Easter — Family — Thanksgiving — Vacation — School — Inspiration, etc.

IDEALS contains no advertising, they are issues of rare beauty and inspiration that you will cherish and keep as a library treasure. We invite you to join our family of SUBSCRIBERS.

IDEALS are published Bi-Monthly

ONE YEAR SUBSCRIPTION — six consecutive issues as published —   only $7.50

**IDEALS PUBLISHING CO.
MILWAUKEE, WISCONSIN**

As You Go Through Life

Ella Wheeler Wilcox

Don't look for the flaws
    as you go through life;
And even when you find them,
It is wise and kind to be somewhat blind
And look for the virtue behind them;
For the cloudiest night
    has a hint of light
Somewhere in its shadows hiding;
It's better by far to hunt for a star
Than the spots on the sun abiding.

The current of life runs ever away
To the bosom of God's great ocean.
Don't set your force
    'gainst the river's course
And think to alter its motion.
Don't waste a curse on the universe,
Remember, it lived before you.
Don't butt at the storm
    with your puny form,
But bend and let it go o'er you.

This world will never adjust itself
To suit your whims to the letter;
Some things must go wrong
    your whole life long,
And the sooner you know it the better.
It is folly to fight with the Infinite,
And go under at last in the wrestle.
The wiser man shapes into God's plan
As the water shapes into a vessel.

BELIEVE IN YOURSELF

By Edgar A. Guest

Believe in yourself! Believe you were made
To do any task without calling for aid.
Believe, without growing too scornfully proud,
That you, as the greatest and least are endowed.
A mind to do thinking, two hands and two eyes
Are all the equipment God gives to the wise.

Believe in yourself! You're divinely designed
And perfectly made for the work of mankind.
This truth you must cling to through danger and pain;
The heights man has reached you can also attain.
Believe to the very last hour, for it's true,
That whatever you will you've been gifted to do.

Believe in yourself and step out unafraid.
By misgivings and doubt be not easily swayed.
You've the right to succeed; the precision of skill
Which betokens the great you can earn if you will!
The wisdom of ages is yours if you'll read.
But you've got to believe in yourself to succeed.

IDEALS ARE LIKE STARS; YOU WILL NOT SUCCEED IN TOUCHING THEM WITH YOUR HANDS, BUT LIKE THE SEAFARING MAN ON THE DESERT OF WATERS, YOU CHOOSE THEM AS YOUR GUIDES, AND FOLLOWING THEM, YOU REACH YOUR DESTINY.

CARL SCHURZ

Today

Ella Wheeler Wilcox

With every rising of the Sun
Think of your life as just begun.

The Past has cancelled and buried deep
All Yesterdays. There let them sleep.

Concern yourself with but Today.
Grasp it, and teach it to obey

Your will and plan. Since time began
Today has been the friend of man.

You and Today! A soul sublime
And the great heritage of time.

With God Himself to bind the twain,
Go forth, brave heart! Attain! Attain!

The Bridge Builder

Will Allen Dromgoogle

An old man going a lone highway,
Came at the evening, cold and gray,
To a chasm vast and deep and wide
Through which was flowing a sullen tide;
The old man crossed in the twilight dim,
The sullen stream held no fears for him;
But he turned when safe on the other side
And built a bridge to span the tide.

"Old man," said a fellow pilgrim near,
"You are wasting strength with building here,
Your journey will end with the ending day;
You never again will pass this way,
You have crossed the chasm deep and wide,
Why build you this bridge at the eventide?"

The builder lifted his old gray head,
"Good friend, in the path I have come," he said
"There followeth after me today
A youth whose feet must pass this way.
This chasm that has been naught to me,
To that fair-haired youth may a pitfall be;
He too must cross in the twilight dim,
Good friend, I am building the bridge for him."

©

The Art of Life

Ira D. Scrogum

"Life, beautifully lived, is an art." Yes, whether we will or not, we are artists. To each has been given, by a benevolent Creator, the raw materials out of which life is made.

When we begin our task of living, these raw materials are in the rough, as a stone just taken from the quarry,—a shapeless mass, often unattractive, and seemingly with very limited possibilities,—awaiting the skill of the master artist.

Michelangelo, the great artist of the Renaissance, once said he could see an angel in the rugged stone on which he was working; and that his task was to liberate it.

This is the business of life; namely, to make out of the rough materials of daily opportunity, the shapeless mass of crude experience, the unpromising failures of the past, a life that is attractive, and beautiful, and of enduring value.

Many are merely dabbling around making some strange monstrosity, some childish caricature, some ludicrously grotesque figure which excites only a sense of humor, or of pathos, because of its incongruity.

Others are content to copy life after a common pattern with no skill of artistry, and no sense of life's true values.

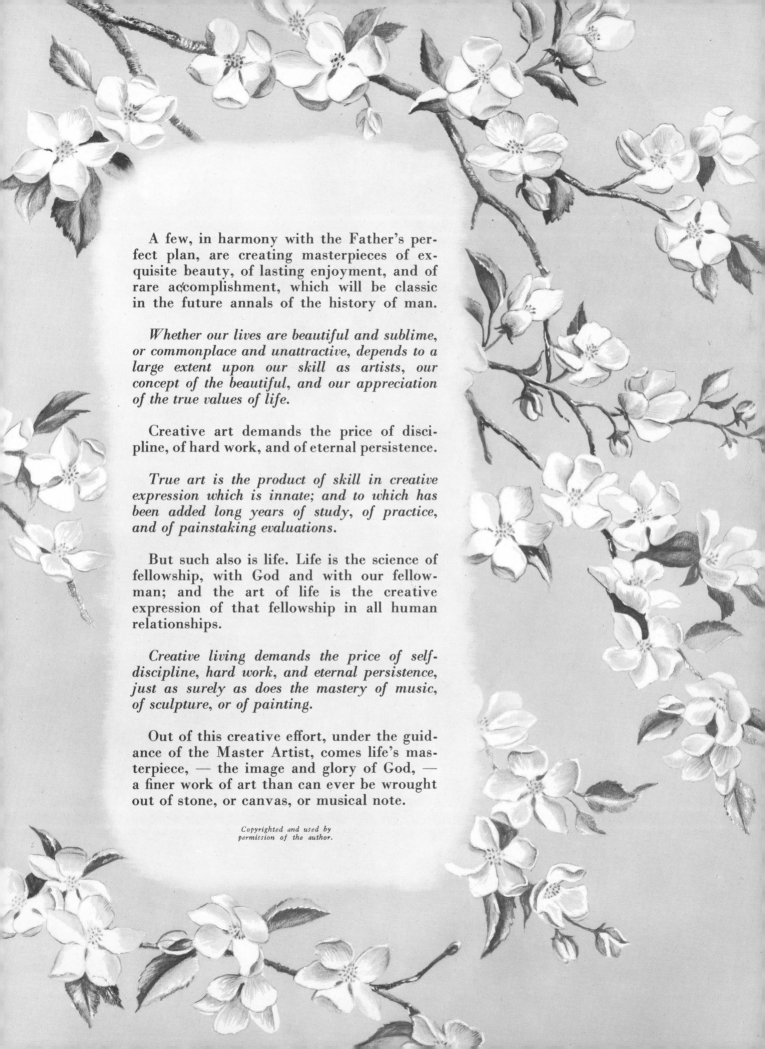

A few, in harmony with the Father's perfect plan, are creating masterpieces of exquisite beauty, of lasting enjoyment, and of rare accomplishment, which will be classic in the future annals of the history of man.

Whether our lives are beautiful and sublime, or commonplace and unattractive, depends to a large extent upon our skill as artists, our concept of the beautiful, and our appreciation of the true values of life.

Creative art demands the price of discipline, of hard work, and of eternal persistence.

True art is the product of skill in creative expression which is innate; and to which has been added long years of study, of practice, and of painstaking evaluations.

But such also is life. Life is the science of fellowship, with God and with our fellow-man; and the art of life is the creative expression of that fellowship in all human relationships.

Creative living demands the price of self-discipline, hard work, and eternal persistence, just as surely as does the mastery of music, of sculpture, or of painting.

Out of this creative effort, under the guidance of the Master Artist, comes life's masterpiece, — the image and glory of God, — a finer work of art than can ever be wrought out of stone, or canvas, or musical note.

To The Dandelion
James Russell Lowell

Dear common flower, that grow'st beside the way,
  Fringing the dusty road with harmless gold,
First pledge of blithesome May,
  Which children pluck, and, full of pride uphold,
High-hearted buccaneers, o'erjoyed that they
  An Eldorado in the grass have found,
Which not the rich earth's ample round
   May match in wealth, thou art more dear to me
   Than all the prouder summer blooms may be.

Gold such as thine ne'er drew the Spanish prow
  Through the primeval hush of Indian seas,
Nor wrinkled the lean brow
  Of age, to rob the lover's heart of ease;
'Tis the spring's largess, which she scatters now
  To rich and poor alike with lavish hand,
Though most hearts never understand
  To take it at God's value, but pass by
  The offered wealth with unrewarded eye.

Then think I of deep shadows on the grass,
  Of meadows where in sun the cattle graze,
Where, as the breezes pass,
  The gleaming rushes lean a thousand ways,
Of leaves that slumber in a cloudy mass,
  Or whiten in the wind, of waters blue
That from the distance sparkle through
  Some woodland gap, and of a sky above
  Where one white cloud like a stray lamb doth move.

My childhood's earliest thoughts are linked with thee;
  The sight of thee calls back the robin's song,
Who, from the dark old tree
  Beside the door, sang clearly all day long,
And I, secure in childish piety,
  Listened as if I heard an angel sing
With news from heaven, which he could bring
  Fresh every day to my untainted ears
  When birds and flowers and I were happy peers.

How like a prodigal doth nature seem,
  When thou, for all thy gold, so common art!
Thou teachest me to deem
  More sacredly of every human heart,
Since each reflects in joy its scanty gleam
  Of heaven, and could some wondrous secret show,
Did we but pay the love we owe,
  And with a child's undoubting wisdom look
  On all these living pages of God's book.

The Old Rugged Cross

Rev. George Bennard 1873–

George Bennard

On a hill far a-way stood an old rug-ged cross, The-

em-blem of suf-f'ring and shame; And I love that old cross where the

dear-est and best For a world of lost sin-ners was slain.

Chorus

So I'll cher-ish the old rug-ged cross, Till my tro-phies at last I lay down; I will

cling to the old rug-ged cross, And ex-change it some day for a crown.

Oh, that old rugged cross, so despised
  by the world
Has a wondrous attraction to me;
For the dear Lamb of God left
  His glory above
To bear it to dark Calvary.

In the old rugged cross, stained
  with blood so divine,
A wondrous beauty I see;
For 'twas on that old cross Jesus
  suffered and died.
To pardon and sanctify me.

To the old rugged cross
I will ever be true,
It's shame and reproach gladly bear;
Then He'll call me some day to
my home far away,
Where His glory forever I'll share.

Jesus, Lover of My Soul

Charles Wesley, 1707-1788

Simeon B. Marsh, 1798-1875

Je-sus, Lov-er of my soul, Let me to thy bos-om fly,

While the near-er wa-ters roll, While the tem-pest still is high:

Hide me, O—my Sav-iour,—hide, Till the storm of life is—past;

Safe in-to the ha-ven guide; O re-ceive my soul at last! A-men.

Other refuge have I none;
  Hangs my helpless soul on Thee;
Leave, ah! leave me not alone,
  Still support and comfort me:
All my trust on Thee is stayed,
  All my help from Thee I bring;
Cover my defenseless head
  With the shadow of Thy wing.

Thou, O Christ, art all I want;
  More than all in Thee I find:
Raise the fallen, cheer the faint,
  Heal the sick, and lead the blind.
Just and holy is Thy Name,
  I am all unrighteousness;
False and full of sin I am,
  Thou art full of truth and grace.

Plenteous grace with Thee is found,
  Grace to cover all my sin;
Let the healing streams abound,
  Make and keep me pure within.
Thou of life the Fountain art,
  Freely let me take of Thee:
Spring Thou up within my heart,
  Rise to all eternity.

Dogwood Tree

Marion Doyle

In May the dogwood blossomed,
And oh, but it was fair;
As if the shimmering whiteness hung
Suspended in the air.

When summer came I passed to find
Its flowering was done,
But lovely still, in silver-green,
It took the morning sun.

And when, in gray November,
Once more with it I stood,
Its little lamps of scarlet tips
Lit all the sombre wood.

It was as if that slender tree
Was a message meant for me:
What if the sky was tarnished metal?
I could recall each pearly petal,

And here were berries flaming bright
As a signal fire at night,
Spelling out against the skies:
Nothing ever wholly dies.

I brought a branch away with me
As a living shibboleth,
A shining promise there shall be,
Out of dark November's death,
White rebirth in a dogwood tree —

And glowing as that branch, my faith
Renewed in immortality.

If Spring came but once in a century, instead of once a year, or burst forth with the sound of an earthquake, and not in silence, what wonder and expectation there would be in all hearts to behold the miraculous change! But now the silent succession suggests nothing but necessity. To most men only the cessation of the miracle would be miraculous, and the perpetual exercise of God's power seems less wonderful than its withdrawal would be.

Longfellow

Our Lord has written the promise of the Resurrection, not in books alone, but in every leaf in springtime.

Luther

Reflect upon your present blessings, of which every man has many; not on your past misfortunes, of which all men have some.

Dickens

To see the world in a grain of sand,
And a heaven in a wild flower;
Hold infinity in the palm of your hand,
And eternity in an hour.

William Blake

So then the year is repeating its old story again. We are come once more, thank God! to its most charming chapter. The violets and the May flowers are as its inscriptions or vignettes. It always makes a pleasant impression on us, when we open again at these pages of the book of life.

Goethe

No man can tell whether he is rich or poor by turning to his ledger. It is the heart that makes a man rich. He is rich according to what he is, not according to what he has.

Henry Ward Beecher

Ring, Easter Bells

Helen A. Holton

Ring, Easter bells, ring merrily
  a welcome to the Spring,
And let your joyful cadence
  a peaceful halo bring.
Fill the wild woods with music,
  let the bluebird gaily trill,
And the robin with his silver notes
  vie with the thrush at will.

Ring, Easter bells, ring cheerily
  a welcome to the flowers,
That peep their heads so shyly
  beneath the woodland bowers.
Call forth the sleeping petals
  where winter's snows have lain,
Ring, Easter bells, ring cheerily,
  for Spring has come again.

Ring, Easter bells, ring joyfully
  the message soft and clear,
Tell that the earth is born anew
  and filled with hope and cheer;
That faith bids all the world
  take up her song of victory.
Ring, Easter bells, from far and near,
  ring out exultingly.

©

In those days came John the Baptist, preaching in the wilderness of Judaea.

And saying, "Repent ye: for the kingdom of heaven is at hand. For this is He that was spoken of by the prophet Esaias, saying, 'The voice of One crying in the wilderness, Prepare ye the way of the Lord, make His paths straight.'"

And the same John had his raiment of camel's hair, and a leathern girdle about his loins; and his meat was locusts and wild honey.

St. Matthew
Chapter III, 1–4

"I indeed baptize you with water unto repentance; but He that cometh after me is mightier than I, Whose shoes I am not worthy to bear: He shall baptize you with the Holy Ghost, and with fire:

"Whose fan is in His hand, and He will thoroughly purge His floor, and gather His wheat into the garner; but He will burn up the chaff with unquenchable fire."

St. Matthew
Chapter III, 11–12

Legend of
The Easter Flower

Grace Mathews Walker

Until the first Easter, the flower known today as the "Easter Lily" was naught but a small white flower, hanging so close to the ground that it scarcely could be seen.

Folk wondered at the strange delicate perfume that often filled the air. Little did they realize that it came from the tiny unseen flower!

Because of a yearning to serve humanity and to share with the world its delicate perfume, it prayed to God to be allowed to become the most beautiful of white flowers. But first it had a real service to perform to prove its worthiness.

As it grew in great abundance in the Garden of Gethsemane, its perfume blessed the Saviour as He knelt in prayer.

In tender solicitude it nestled close to the cross of Calvary as the Saviour hung there. Because of its sympathetic, understanding love the plant grew to its full height, and the tender white blossom looked up into the Saviour's face.

The purity of its face, the sweetness of its character, the meekness of its life were shared in mute understanding by the Man of Galilee.

The strange celestial beauty of the tiny flower comforted the women at the cross. To them it seemed to breathe the very message of immortality.

A tiny white bud smothering beneath the green leaves grew near the Saviour's tomb. For three days it struggled to lift its blossom up to the great stone that closed the opening of the sepulcher. Weighted down with grief, its struggles seemed in vain. Then at Easter dawn its prayer was answered!

In the glory of the Resurrection — where'er the footsteps of the Saviour pressed the tiny bud to earth — the Easter Lily sprang to birth!

Today it is the symbol of purity; and as it breathes its sweet fragrance on the air, it breathes the story of the Resurrection to all mankind — a story of immortality to all the world!

It is as delightful to the eye as cool water to thirsty lips; as refreshing as the first warm day of spring; as radiant as the light from heaven; as pure and as innocent as the Babe of Bethlehem.

In its presence, creeds — like robes — are laid aside; and with the tragedy of the cross behind, we face the Easter dawn and the assurance of everlasting life!

A Trip to Easter Bunny Land

by Ritchie T. Weikel

Where does the Easter Bunny go,
When Winter comes with ice and snow?
What does he do the whole year through?
I often wondered just like you,
Until one day I came upon
An Irish elf called Lepricon,
Who, learnin' my name is Patty O'Shay,
Kindly offered to show me the way
To that magic place of great renown,
Known as Easter Bunny Town.
We walked tiptoe, without a sound,
Down a path far underground
To a tiny door and sign so grand
"Welcome to Easter Bunny Land."
So we went right in with no trouble at all,
For I quickly became only two feet tall.
There was Bunny and all his crew
Much too busy to say, "Howdy do!"
Oh, there was hustle, bustle and scurry,
And I heard Bunny call, "Do please hurry!
The eggs must be boiled until just right;
Painted with colors gay and bright,
Then in boxes and baskets they go,
For little friends that we all know.
So, kind helpers, we cannot play,
We must be ready before Easter Day!"
I turned to my guide, but just as I feared,
That mischievous elf had disappeared.
Then I felt sleepy, and what do you think?
I awoke in bed, quick as a wink!

The Magic Pool

by
Dorothy Weiner

The bunnies were dressed in their furry coats
Neatly donned for the Easter parade,
And going along in gay little carts
Were the eggs they diligently made.

The eggs were dyed from a rainbow that dripped
Down at Bunnyville's rock garden pond,
And I don't think it could be managed at all
Without the magic of some fairy's wand.

They dipped, they splashed and they splattered about
Till the rainbow was completely dissolved,
But they never gave up until they were through
For they were too deeply involved.

Then they dressed up in their furry best
And hopped off as bunnies will do,
To cart off their art to the parade —
Easter eggs dipped in rainbow hue.

I'm thankful for all good with which
I've been blessed throughout life.
For hardships, and for heartaches, too,
For failures, trials and strife.
I'm thankful for each little prayer
Someone has said for me;
For loving thoughts, for friendliness,
For all good will I see.

My thanks for hands, with which I could
Serve someone on life's way;
For all small deeds of kindness
I'm allowed to do each day.
I'm thankful for all happiness,
Each long hour of deep sorrow;
God thus in His great mercy gives
More wisdom for tomorrow.

A. R. Gronros ©

Summer Days Are Here Again!

P. F. Freeman

When the leaves are brightest green,
And flowers bloom everywhere,
When beauties of nature can be seen
As scented fragrance fills the air —
    Summer days are here again.

When sunbeams of an early dawn
Lend beauty to a sparkling dew,
And the sunrise of another morn
Softly blends with skies of blue —
    Summer days are here again.

When joy and happiness fill the soul,
And Cupid's works are not in vain,
When hand-in-hand true lovers stroll
In the shade of lover's lane —
    Summer days are here again.

When there's action at the swimming hole,
And vacation is not a dream,
When the fisherman takes his fishing pole
And starts out for the nearest stream —
    Summer days are here again.

When window shades are securely drawn,
And childish patter is heard no more,
When papers lay strewn upon the lawn
And there's nobody home next door —
    Summer days are here again.

On Mother's Day

As years ago we carried to your knees
The tales and treasures of eventful days,
Knowing no deed too humble for your praise,
Nor any gift too trivial to please,
So, still we bring — with older smiles and tears —
What gifts we may, to claim the old, dear right;
Your faith, beyond the silence and the night,
Your love still close and watching through the years.

Written by Kathleen Norris, 1911

Time To Go Fishing

Edgar A. Guest

Time to go fishing; to sit in a
   boat
Or wade in a stream,
To wear an old hat, an old shirt
   and no coat
And maybe dream.

Time to go fishing; away from
   the town,
Its stress and its strain,
To depart from the shore, every
   burden put down,
And be humble again.

Time to go fishing; pride's
   vestments to leave
On a hook or a shelf,
To drop all the shams that so
   often deceive
And just be yourself.

Time to go fishing; no matter the
   spot
Or sunshine or rain,
And return to the town, whether
   lucky or not,
To brave life again.

The One That Got Away

P. F. Freeman

When fishin' season's in full swing,
There are lots of tales to tell,
A few that oft' a smile will bring
When put over fairly well.
Tall fishin' stories have long been told
An' it's human so they say,
For man to brag in manner bold
'Bout the fish that got away.

There are fish that bite a hook
An' to danger give no thought;
Fish that stop to take a look,
An' are not so easily caught;
Some of them are more than wise,
Others with worms will never play,
Won't snap at flies that are disguis'd,
But will calmly swim away.

A fish that's held in the hand
Rates more than those in the stream,
For few are ever brought to land
Like those of which we dream.
Fishermen oft' will growl an' fret
With lots of temper to display,
For never was a fish caught yet
Like the one that got away.

Woodland Cathedral

Patience Strong

Go into the woodlands if you seek for peace of mind — at this time when Nature's mood is gentle, quiet and kind . . . When soft winds fan the trembling leaves about the cloistered glade — and paths go winding deep into the green and breathless shade.

Where nothing breaks the silence of the warm and fragrant air — but snatches of sweet melody . . . and wings that rend and tear — the stillness of the windless dells where shallow brooklets flow — and shadows fleck the water as the sunbeams come and go.

An unseen Presence walks the woods . . . A sense of holy things — haunts the dim Cathedral aisles; and every bird that sings — is like some morning chorister, and every breath of air — seems to bring the secret murmur of a whispered prayer.

©

In the Forest

Patience Strong

In the forest we can rise
above our worldly care;
in the forest we may find
tranquillity, and share
— the silence and the
secret strength of great
and ancient trees —
sturdy oaks and silver
birches, laughing in the
breeze.

In the forest we can learn
life's lessons if we will;
how to turn towards
the sunshine, standing
straight and still — how
to be content with slow
development—and grow,
in grace and strength in
spite of storms, of wind
and frost and snow . . .
Countless birds and in-
sects seek protection in
the tree — food and
shelter; isn't this true
hospitality? And when
winds have stripped the
branches of their sum-
mer dress — they survive
to show the world new
forms of loveliness.

Stately tree! Look down
on me — and teach me
how to be — Strong and
wise — To live my days
in quiet dignity . . . In
the forest silences our
petty warfares cease. In
God's own cathedral
we discover Truth and
Peace.

©

Her Announcement

Frank Carleton Nelson

Time's been passing swiftly
And the day is here right now
When I ought to write about it,
But it seems I don't know how;
For in words I can't describe it
And my verses won't express
Her great anticipation and
Her sweetest happiness,
As today she makes announcement
Of her wedding that's to be,
With a heart that's overflowing
With life's grandest ecstasy.

Though it breaks the family circle
And it leaves an empty chair,
'Tis not the time for grieving,
For there's gladness everywhere,
The birds are singing sweeter
Than they have for years, it seems,
And the flowers in the garden
Bend to listen to her dreams,
And the sun comes out the stronger
And its brightest rays it sends,
Just to cheer the great announcement
She is making to her friends.

So, we join the celebration,
As she stands outside the gate,
That opens to the pathway
Where the greater charms await,
May she know life's sweetest blessings,
As she journeys down the way,
And the joy be everlasting
That she's tasting of today,
May the road be hedged with roses,
As they travel hand-in-hand,
With the romance never-ending
Till they reach the border-land.

At the Altar

Winn E. McGowan

At the altar of marriage together they stand,
  Hearts in unison, hand-in-hand,
Thinking the thoughts too deep to say,
  Dreaming the dreams of their wedding day.

Oh, pilgrims, new to this way of life,
  Starting your journey as husband and wife,
Lost in the bliss of the golden now,
  Will you always remember your wedding vow?

The future before you, you cannot see;
  But 'tis yours to make it what it will be.
Will you keep your promise your whole life through?
  Had you thought of that when you said, "I do"?

Are you dreaming of pleasure unmixed with pain,
  Or of loss and sorrow, as well as gain?
Remember your promise "for better or worse,"
  For the fruit of this day may be blessing or curse.

For marriage means body, and heart, and soul;
  'Tis the song of a lifetime, perfect and whole;
A life of devotion, tender and true,
  Was that what you meant when you said "I do"?

The Best Part of a Vacation!

Olive Weaver Ridenour

The best part of vacation,
Though far and wide we roam,
Is when it's time to travel back
The trail that leads to home.
Strange roads and ways are thrilling
And mighty fine to see,
But when vacation's over
At home we long to be.

*It's fine to see the wonders
And beauties of the land —
The mighty snow-capped mountains,
The rolling sea, the sand,
The city's man-made glory;
But when tired we have grown,
We turn our faces toward
The path that leads to home.*

It's fine to see the north land,
The mountains of the west,
The great southern plantations,
But, somehow, I love best
Of all the towns and cities,
Though far and wide we roam,
That little rambling village
At trail's end we call . . . home!

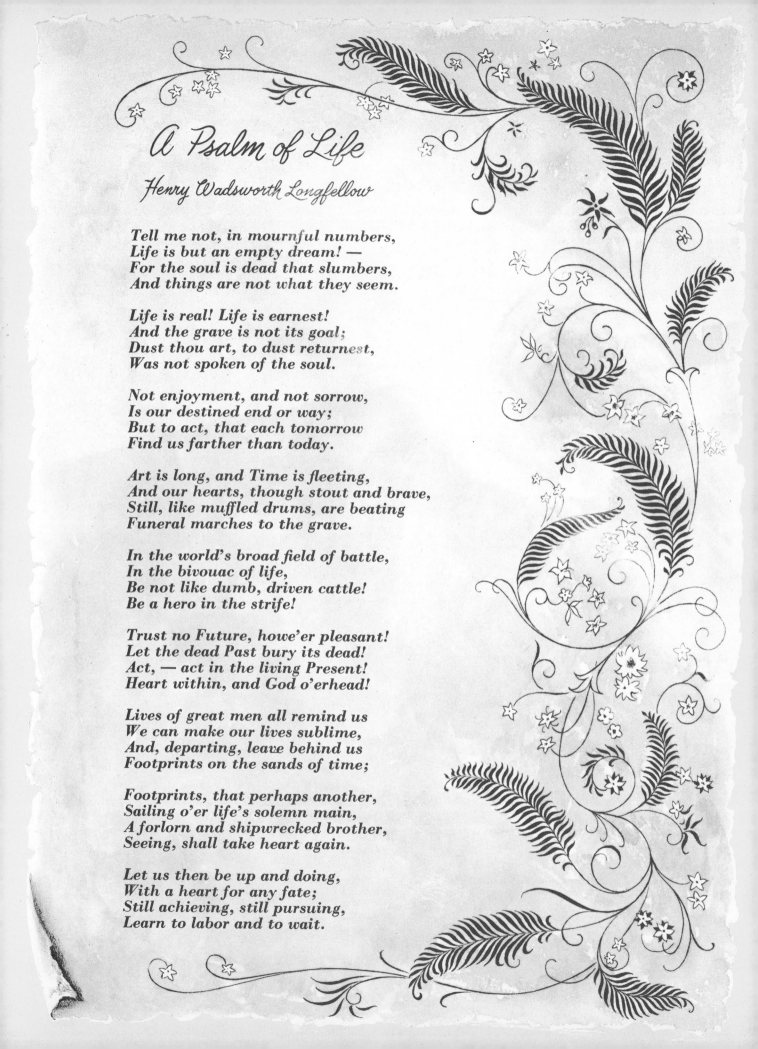

A Psalm of Life

Henry Wadsworth Longfellow

Tell me not, in mournful numbers,
Life is but an empty dream! —
For the soul is dead that slumbers,
And things are not what they seem.

Life is real! Life is earnest!
And the grave is not its goal;
Dust thou art, to dust returnest,
Was not spoken of the soul.

Not enjoyment, and not sorrow,
Is our destined end or way;
But to act, that each tomorrow
Find us farther than today.

Art is long, and Time is fleeting,
And our hearts, though stout and brave,
Still, like muffled drums, are beating
Funeral marches to the grave.

In the world's broad field of battle,
In the bivouac of life,
Be not like dumb, driven cattle!
Be a hero in the strife!

Trust no Future, howe'er pleasant!
Let the dead Past bury its dead!
Act, — act in the living Present!
Heart within, and God o'erhead!

Lives of great men all remind us
We can make our lives sublime,
And, departing, leave behind us
Footprints on the sands of time;

Footprints, that perhaps another,
Sailing o'er life's solemn main,
A forlorn and shipwrecked brother,
Seeing, shall take heart again.

Let us then be up and doing,
With a heart for any fate;
Still achieving, still pursuing,
Learn to labor and to wait.

He Was Everybody—Grown A Little Taller

Let's skip all the things you've read about him, all the things you heard too often or too young.

Forget the face on the penny, the statue in Washington, the Emancipation Proclamation, the speech at Gettysburg. Forget the official things and look at the big thing.

Why do we love this man, dead long before our time, yet dear to us as a father? What was there about Abraham Lincoln?

He came out of nowhere special — a cabin like any other out West. His folks were nobody special — pleasant, hard-working people like many others. Abe was a smart boy, but not too smart. He could do a good day's work on the farm, though he'd just as soon stand around and talk. He told funny stories. He was strong and kind. He'd never try to hurt you, or cheat you, or fool you.

Young Abe worked at odd jobs and read law books at night. Eventually he found his way into local politics. And it was then that people, listening to his speeches, began to know there was something special about Abe Lincoln.

Abe talked about running a country as if it were something you could do. It was just a matter of people getting along.

He had nothing against anybody, rich or poor, who went his own way and let the other fellow go his. No matter how mixed up things got, Abe made you feel that the answer was somewhere among those old rules that everybody knows: no hurting, no cheating, no fooling.

Abe had a way of growing without changing. So it seemed perfectly natural to find him in the White House one day, padding around in his slippers, putting his feet on a chair when he had a deep one to think about — the same Abe Lincoln he'd always been, and yet the most dignified and the strongest and the steadiest man anybody had ever known. And when that terrible war came that might have torn his country apart, no one doubted what Abe would do. He was a family man; he resolved to keep the American family together.

Abe Lincoln always did what most people would have done, said what most people wanted said, thought what most people thought when they stopped to think about it. He was everybody, grown a little taller — the warm and living proof of our American faith that greatness comes out of everywhere when it is free to come.

Reprinted through the courtesy of
John Hancock Mutual Life Insurance Company.

Twenty-Third Psalm

Bible: Psalm, 23

The Lord is my shepherd; I shall not want.
He maketh me to lie down in green pastures:
He leadeth me beside the still waters.
He restoreth my soul:
He leadeth me in the paths of righteousness
   for His name's sake.

Yea, though I walk through the valley of the
   shadow of death, I will fear no evil:
For thou art with me; thy rod and thy staff
   they comfort me.
Thou preparest a table before me in the
   presence of mine enemies:
Thou anointest my head with oil; my cup
   runneth over.
Surely goodness and mercy shall follow me all
   the days of my life:
And I will dwell in the house of the Lord for ever.

It Takes a Heap o' Livin'

Edgar A. Guest

It takes a heap o' livin' in
  a house t' make it home,
A heap o' sun an' shadder,
  an' ye sometimes have t' roam
Afore ye really 'preciate
  the things ye lef' behind,
An' hunger fer 'em somehow
  with 'em allus on yer mind.

It don't make any difference
  how rich ye get t' be,
How much yer chairs an' tables cost,
  how great yer luxury,
It ain't home t' ye, though it be
  the palace of a king,
Until somehow yer soul is
  sort o' wrapped 'round everything.

Home ain't a place that gold can buy
  or get up in a minute;
Afore it's home there's got t' be
  a heap o' livin' in it;
Within the walls there's got t' be
  some babies born, and then
Right there ye've got t' bring 'em up
  t' women good, an' men;

And gradjerly, as time goes on,
  ye find ye wouldn't part
With anything they ever used—
  they've grown into yer heart:
The old high chairs, the playthings, too,
  the little shoes they wore
Ye hoard; an' if ye could ye'd keep
  the thumbmarks on the door.

Ye've got t' sing an' dance fer years,
  ye've got t' romp an' play,
An' learn t' love the things ye have
  by usin' 'em each day;
Even the roses 'round the porch
  must blossom year by year
Afore they 'come a part o' ye,
  Suggestin' someone dear

Who used t' love 'em long ago,
  an' trained 'em jes' t' run
The way they do, so's they would
  get the early mornin' sun;
Ye've got t' love each brick an' stone
  from cellar up t' dome;
It takes a heap o' livin'
  in a house to make it home.

We Thank Thee

John Oxenham

For all things beautiful,
  and good, and true;
For things that seemed not good
  yet turned to good;

For all the sweet
  compulsions of Thy will
That chastened, tried,
  and wrought us to Thy shape;

For things unnumbered
  that we take of right,
And value first
  when they are withheld;

For light and air;
  sweet sense of sound and smell;
For ears to hear
  the heavenly harmonies;

For eyes to see
  the unseen in the seen;
For vision of the
  Worker in the work;

For hearts to apprehend
  Thee everywhere —
We thank Thee, Lord.

©

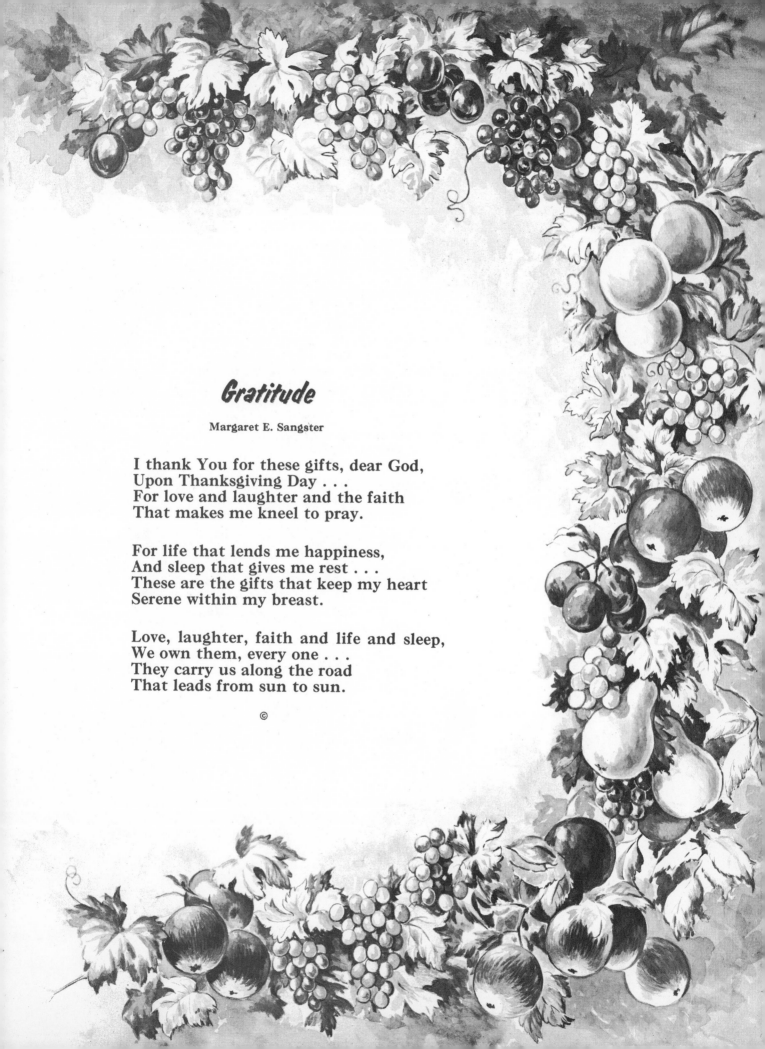

Gratitude

Margaret E. Sangster

I thank You for these gifts, dear God,
Upon Thanksgiving Day . . .
For love and laughter and the faith
That makes me kneel to pray.

For life that lends me happiness,
And sleep that gives me rest . . .
These are the gifts that keep my heart
Serene within my breast.

Love, laughter, faith and life and sleep,
We own them, every one . . .
They carry us along the road
That leads from sun to sun.

©

It's a long Way....

R. Armistead Grady

It is a long way home from school for a little lad only five, going on six. Going to school, in the morning, he is gay and fresh and, besides, he has the company of other children, but coming home he has no companions and must walk alone, and the way is very long. So, his Mother has been going part way to meet him and together they walk home, hand in hand.

"Be sure to come to meet me, Mother," I heard him say this morning as he started out — so little and so young — to school. "It's not so far and I don't get tired when you come part way to meet me."

When the road is long, the journey rough, and the wayfarer weary, how lovely it is to be met part way and the last steps home made easy and the journey shortened.

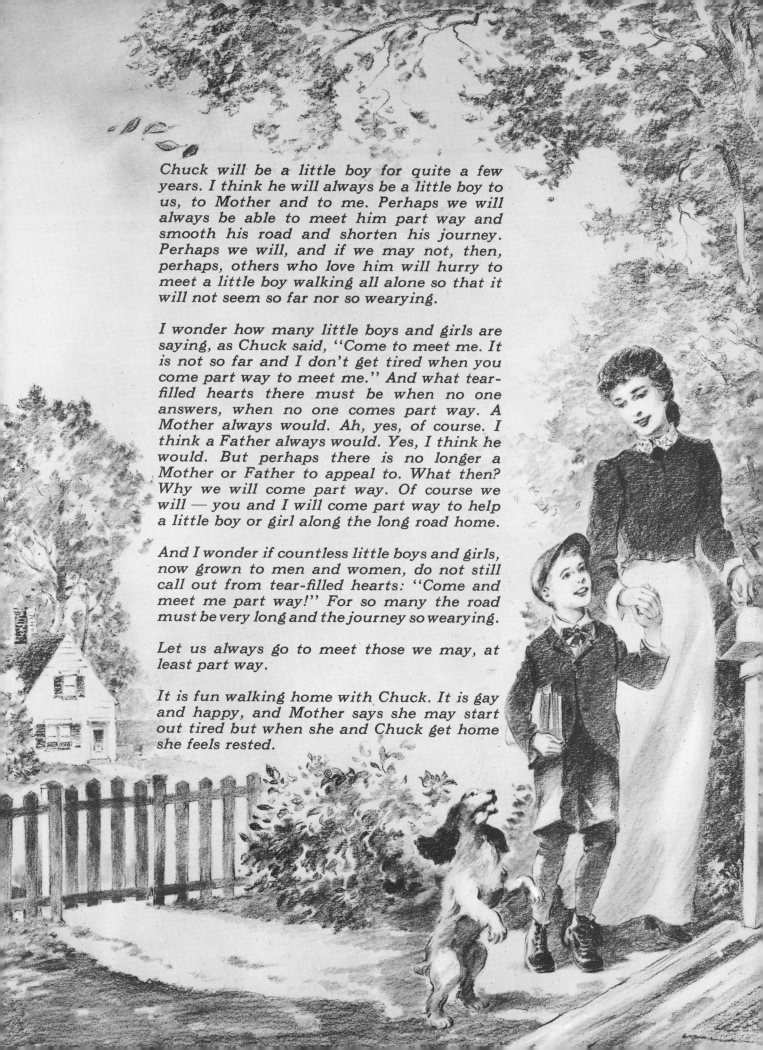

Chuck will be a little boy for quite a few years. I think he will always be a little boy to us, to Mother and to me. Perhaps we will always be able to meet him part way and smooth his road and shorten his journey. Perhaps we will, and if we may not, then, perhaps, others who love him will hurry to meet a little boy walking all alone so that it will not seem so far nor so wearying.

I wonder how many little boys and girls are saying, as Chuck said, "Come to meet me. It is not so far and I don't get tired when you come part way to meet me." And what tear-filled hearts there must be when no one answers, when no one comes part way. A Mother always would. Ah, yes, of course. I think a Father always would. Yes, I think he would. But perhaps there is no longer a Mother or Father to appeal to. What then? Why we will come part way. Of course we will — you and I will come part way to help a little boy or girl along the long road home.

And I wonder if countless little boys and girls, now grown to men and women, do not still call out from tear-filled hearts: "Come and meet me part way!" For so many the road must be very long and the journey so wearying.

Let us always go to meet those we may, at least part way.

It is fun walking home with Chuck. It is gay and happy, and Mother says she may start out tired but when she and Chuck get home she feels rested.

Teach Him Gently... if you can...

Dan Valentine

My young son starts to school tomorrow . . . It's all going to be strange and new to him for a while, and I wish you would sort of treat him gently. . .

You see, up to now, he's been our little boy.

He's been boss of the back yard . . . His mother has always been around to repair his wounds, and I've always been handy to soothe his feelings.

But now, things are going to be different . . .

This morning he's going to walk down the front steps, wave his hand, and start out on the great adventure . . . It's an adventure that will probably include wars and tragedy and sorrow.

To live his life in the world he will live in requires faith and love and courage.

So, world, I wish you would sort of take him by his young hand and teach him the things he will have to know.

Teach him, but gently . . . if you can.

He will have to learn, I know, that all men are not just, that all men are not true.

But teach him also that for every scoundrel there is a hero . . . that for every selfish politician, there is a dedicated leader . . . Teach him that for every enemy, there is a friend.

It will take time, world, I know, but teach him, if you can, that a nickel earned is of far more value than a dollar found . . . Teach him to learn to lose . . . and to enjoy winning.

Steer him away from envy, if you can, and teach him the secret of quiet laughter.

Let him learn early that the bullies are the easiest people to lick . . . Teach him if you can, the wonder of books . . . But also give him quiet time to ponder the eternal mystery of birds in the sky, bees in the sun, and flowers on a green hillside.

In school, world, teach him it is far more honorable to fail than to cheat . . . Teach him to have faith in his own ideas, even if everyone tells him they are wrong . . . Teach him to be gentle with gentle people and tough with tough people.

Try to give my son the strength not to follow the crowd when everyone else is getting on the band wagon . . . Teach him to listen to all men . . . but teach him also to filter all he hears on a screen of truth and take only the good that comes through.

Teach him, if you can, how to laugh when he is sad . . . Teach him there is no shame in tears . . . Teach him there can be glory in failure and despair in success.

Teach him to scoff at cynics and to beware of too much sweetness . . . Teach him to sell his brawn and brains to the highest bidders but never to put a price tag on his heart and soul.

Teach him to close his ears to a howling mob . . . and to stand and fight if he thinks he's right.

Treat him gently, world, but don't coddle him, because only the test of fire makes fine steel.

Let him have the courage to be impatient . . . let him have the patience to be brave.

Teach him always to have sublime faith in himself. Because then he will always have sublime faith in mankind.

This is a big order, world, but see what you can do . . . He's such a fine little fellow, my son!

Autumn Tapestry

Ruth G. Newman

With just a whisper of wintry chill,
And a sprinkling of frost-diamonds over the hill,
A blazing new sun in the blue sky above,
Autumn has come to the mountains I love.

The mountains are vistas of beauty untold:
Warm shades of burgundy, red, green, and gold.
Leaves of all colors come scurrying by,
Racing the clouds that scamper on high.

The white of a church spire, meadows of brown,
Hills misty purple, with clouds for a crown;
God shows us beauty in so many ways,
Each golden moment of bright autumn days.

©

Thanksgiving Day

Lydia Maria Child
(1802-1880)

Over the river and through the wood,
   To Grandfather's house we go;
      The horse knows the way
      To carry the sleigh
   Through the white and drifted snow.

Over the river and through the wood —
   Oh, how the wind does blow!
      It stings the toes
      And bites the nose,
   As over the ground we go.

Over the river and through the wood,
   To have a first-rate play.
      Hear the bells ring,
      "Ting-a-ling-ding!"
   Hurrah for Thanksgiving Day!

Over the river and through the wood,
    Trot fast, my dapple-gray!
        Spring over the ground,
        Like a hunting-hound!
    For this is Thanksgiving Day.

Over the river and through the wood,
    And straight through the barnyard gate.
        We seem to go
        Extremely slow —
    It is so hard to wait!

Over the river and through the wood —
    Now Grandmother's cap I spy!
        Hurrah for the fun!
        Is the pudding done?
    Hurrah for the pumpkin pie!

Autumn Is Here

Edgar Daniel Kramer

Mist in the meadows,
   Flame on the hills,
Withered leaves dancing
   Down woodland rills,
Partridges piping
   Shrilly and clear,
And we are knowing
   Autumn is here!

Fat pumpkins staring
   Up at the sky,
Goldenrod flouting
   Winds that dance by,
Poplars and birches
   Trembling and sere,
And we are knowing
   Autumn is here!

Purple grapes flaming
   Up from the earth,
Scarlet sage mocking
   Winter's harsh mirth,
Goose flying southward
   Over the weir,
And we are knowing
   Autumn is here!

Chestnuts and shellbarks
   Leaving the trees,
Squirrels and chipmunks
   Busy as bees,
Blazing log-fires
   Giving us cheer,
And we are knowing
   Autumn is here!

A Dog
and
A Kid
•
Berton Braley

No one will invent and no one ever did . . . a happier pair than a dog and a kid . . .
For doubt can't bedim nor can worry befog . . . the gay zestful way of a kid and a
dog . . . Athrob with adventure, their hearts beat as one . . . Their pulses resurge
with the rhythm of fun . . . They swing into action as impulse may bid . . . "Today
is the day" for a dog and a kid . . . Oh God, clear the pathway along which they
jog . . . And smooth out the bumps for a kid and his dog . . . And make of the world
that they wander amid . . . A place truly fit for a dog and a kid.

Little Shoes

Barton Rees Pogue

There are little coats and caps and hoods
Around our house these days,
There are little dresses, gowns and shirts
For which a father pays!
But somehow of the things there are
That little babies use,
I seem to notice most of all
Her little soft-sole shoes.

I see them every night there on the bench,
Atop her pile of clothes,
Like little boats a-riding waves
A pleasant sea-wind blows,
And yet not boats out on the deep,
For in the toes there wink
At me some quite big holes would make
Them fill with sea and sink.

I pick them up and muse a while,
I turn them up and down,
Those little boots of buttoned-black
With soles so soft and brown.
Much nearer do they come to me
Than anything she wears,
They seem to solemnize my thoughts
And call me to my prayers.

I wonder why they lure me so,
What power do they possess
To make a strong man stand and dream?
I cannot even guess,
But somehow of the things she has,
That little babies use,
I love and cherish most of all
Those little soft-sole shoes.

THE ROAD AHEAD

I think that human life is much like road life. You stand on a hill, and look down and across the valley, and another prodigious hill lifts itself upon the other side. The day is hot, your horse is weary, and you are tired; and it seems to you that you cannot climb that long hill. But you had better trot down the hill you are on, and not trouble yourself about the other one. You find the valley pleasant and inspiring. When you get across it, you meet only a slight ascent, and begin to wonder where the steep hill is which you saw. You drive along briskly, and when you reach the highest point, you find that there has not been an inch of the hill over which you have not trotted. You see that it was illusory. The slight ascent looked almost like a perpendicular steep; but when you come to pass over it, step by step, you find it to be a good traveling road.

So it is with your troubles. Just in that way your anticipations of mischief hang before you; and when you come to where they are, you find them to be all smooth turnpikes. Men ought to be ashamed, after they have done that two or three times, not to take the hint, and profit by it; yet they will not. They will suffer from anticipated troubles just as much as though they had no such experience. They have not wit enough to make use of the lesson which their life is continually teaching them; namely, that a large majority of the troubles which they worry themselves about beforehand either never come or are easily borne. They form a habit of fretting about future troubles. It was not the old monks alone who wore sackcloth and hair shirts; you wear them as much as they did; only you wear them inside, while they wore them outside — you wear them in your heart, they wore them on their skins. They were wiser than you are.

Henry Ward Beecher

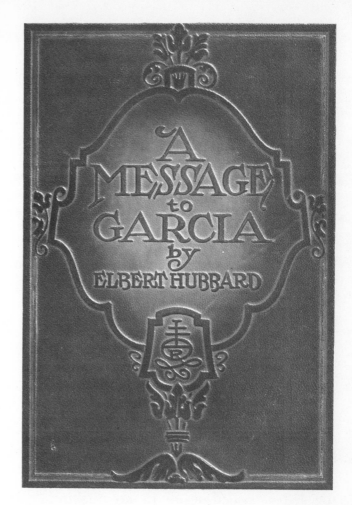

❧ This literary trifle "A Message to Garcia," was written one evening after supper, in a single hour. It was on the Twenty-second of February, Eighteen Hundred Ninety-nine, Washington's Birthday, and we were just going to press with the March "Philistine." The thing leaped hot from my heart, written after a trying day. ❧ ❧

❧ The immediate suggestion, though, came from a little argument over the teacups, when my boy Bert suggested that Rowan was the real hero of the Cuban War. Rowan had gone alone and done the thing—carried the message to Garcia. ❧ ❧

❧ It came to me like a flash! Yes, the boy is right, the hero is the man who does his work—who carries the message to Garcia. I got up from the table, and wrote "A Message to Garcia." I thought so little of it that we ran it in the Magazine without a heading. ❧

❧ Over forty million copies of "A Message to Garcia" have been printed. ❧ ❧

❧ This is said to be a larger circulation than any other literary venture has ever attained during the lifetime of the author, in all history. ❧ ❧ —Elbert Hubbard

_____

❧ Prior to the author's death in 1915—he was lost in the tragic sinking of the Lusitania—over forty million copies of this "literary trifle" were printed and sold. ❧ ❧

❧ It has been acclaimed by many as the most outstanding business inspirational writing of all times. ❧ ❧

I
N ALL this Cuban business there is one man stands out on the horizon of my memory like Mars at perihelion.

¶ When war broke out between Spain and the United States, it was very necessary to communicate quickly with the leader of the Insurgents. Garcia was somewhere in the mountain fastnesses of Cuba—no one knew where. No mail or telegraph message could reach him. The President must secure his co-operation, and quickly. What to do!

¶ Some one said to the President, "There is a fellow by the name of Rowan will find Garcia for you, if anybody can." Rowan was sent for and was given a letter to be delivered to Garcia. How "the fellow by the name of Rowan" took the letter, sealed it up in an oilskin pouch, strapped it over his heart, in four days landed by night off the coast of Cuba from an open boat, disappeared into the jungle, and in three weeks came out on the other side of the Island, having traversed a hostile country on foot, and delivered his letter to Garcia—are things I have no special desire to tell in detail.

¶ The point that I wish to make is this: McKinley gave Rowan a letter to be delivered to Garcia; Rowan took the letter and did not ask, "Where is he at?" By the Eternal! there is a man whose form should be cast in deathless bronze and the statue placed in every college of the land. It is not book-learning young men need, nor instruction about this and that, but a stiffening of the vertebrae which will cause them to be loyal to a trust, to act promptly, concentrate their energies: do the thing—"Carry a message to Garcia."

¶ General Garcia is dead now, but there are other Garcias.

¶ No man who has endeavored to carry out an enterprise where many hands were needed, but has been well-nigh appalled at times by the imbecility of the average man—the inability or unwillingness to concentrate on a thing and do it.

¶ Slipshod assistance, foolish inattention, dowdy indifference, and half-hearted work seem the rule; and no man succeeds, unless by hook or crook or threat he forces or bribes other men to assist him; or mayhap, God in His goodness performs a miracle, and sends him an Angel of Light for an assistant. You, reader, put this matter to a test: You are sitting now in your office—six clerks are within call. Summon any one and make this request: "Please look in the encyclopedia and make a brief memorandum for me concerning the life of Correggio."

¶ Will the clerk quietly say, "Yes sir," and go do the task? On your life he will not. He will look at you out of a fishy eye and ask one or more of the following questions:
Who was he?
Which encyclopedia?
Where is the encyclopedia?
Was I hired for that?
Don't you mean Bismarck?

What's the matter with Charlie doing it?
Is he dead?
Is there any hurry?
Shall I bring you the book and let you look it up yourself?
What do you want to know for?

¶ And I will lay you ten to one that after you have answered the questions, and explained how to find the information, and why you want it, the clerk will go off and get one of the other clerks to help him try to find Garcia—and then come back and tell you there is no such man. Of course I may lose my bet, but according to the Law of Average I will not.

¶ Now, if you are wise, you will not bother to explain to your "assistant" that Correggio is indexed under the C's, not in the K's, but you will smile very sweetly and say, "Never mind," and go look it up yourself.

¶ And this incapacity for independent action, this moral stupidity, this infirmity of the will, this unwillingness to cheerfully catch hold and lift—these are the things that put pure Socialism so far into the future. If men will not act for themselves, what will they do when the benefit of their effort is for all? A first mate with knotted club seems necessary; and the dread of getting "the bounce" Saturday night holds many a worker to his place.

¶ Advertise for a stenographer, and nine out of ten who apply can neither spell nor punctuate—and do not think it necessary to.

¶ Can such a one write a letter to Garcia? "You see that bookkeeper," said a foreman to me in a large factory. "Yes; what about him?" "Well, he's a fine accountant, but if I'd send him up-town on an errand, he might accomplish the errand all right, and on the other hand, might stop at four saloons on the way, and when he got to Main Street would forget what he had been sent for." Can such a man be entrusted to carry a message to Garcia?

¶ We have recently been hearing much maudlin sympathy expressed for the "downtrodden denizens of the sweatshop" and the "homeless wanderer searching for honest employment," and with it all often go many hard words for the men in power.

¶ Nothing is said about the employer who grows old before his time in a vain attempt to get frowsy ne'er-do-wells to do intelligent work; and his long, patient striving with "help" that does nothing but loaf when his back is turned. In every store and factory there is a constant weeding-out process going on. The employer is continually sending away "help" that have shown their incapacity to further the interests of the business, and others are being taken on.

¶ No matter how good times are, this sorting continues: only if times are hard and work is scarce, the sorting is done finer—but out and forever out the incompetent and unworthy go. It is the survival of the fittest. Self-interest prompts every employer to keep the best—those who can carry a message to Garcia. ⚜ ⚜

¶ I know one man of really brilliant parts who has not the ability to manage a business of his own, and yet who is absolutely worthless to any one else, because he carries with him constantly the insane suspicion that his employer is oppressing, or intending to oppress, him. He can not give orders; and he will not receive them. ⚜ ⚜

¶ Should a message be given him to take to Garcia, his answer would probably be, "Take it yourself!" ⚜ ⚜

¶ Tonight this man walks the streets looking for work, the wind whistling through his threadbare coat. No one who knows him dare employ him, for he is a regular firebrand of discontent. He is impervious to reason, and the only thing that can impress him is the toe of a thick-soled Number Nine boot.

¶ Of course I know that one so morally deformed is no less to be pitied than a physical cripple; but in our pitying let us drop a tear, too, for the men who are striving to carry on a great enterprise, whose working hours are not limited by the whistle, and whose hair is fast turning white through the struggle to hold in line dowdy indifference, slip-shod imbecility, and the heartless ingratitude which, but for their enterprise, would be both hungry and homeless.

¶ Have I put the matter too strongly? Possibly I have; but when all the world has gone a-slumming I wish to speak a word of sympathy for the man who succeeds—the man who, against great odds, has directed the efforts of others, and having succeeded, finds there's nothing in it: nothing but bare board and clothes. I have carried a dinner-pail and worked for day's wages, and I have also been an employer of labor, and I know there is something to be said on both sides. There is no excellence, per se, in poverty; rags are no recommendation; and all employers are not rapacious and high-handed, any more than all poor men are virtuous. ⚜ ⚜

¶ My heart goes out to the man who does his work when the "boss" is away, as well as when he is at home. And the man who, when given a letter for Garcia, quietly takes the missive, without asking any idiotic questions, and with no lurking intention of chucking it into the nearest sewer, or of doing aught else but deliver it, never gets "laid off," nor has to go on a strike for higher wages. Civilization is one long anxious search for just such individuals. Anything such a man asks shall be granted. His kind is so rare that no employer can afford to let him go. He is wanted in every city, town and village—in every office, shop, store and factory. ⚜ ⚜

¶ The world cries out for such: he is needed, and needed badly — the man who can carry A MESSAGE TO GARCIA. ⚜ ⚜

Outlook

Priscilla Leonard

Forget each kindness that you do
  As soon as you have done it.
Forget the praise that falls to you
  The moment you have won it.
Forget the slander that you hear
  Before you can repeat it.
Forget each slight, each spite, each sneer
  Wherever you may meet it.

Remember every kindness done
  To you, whate'er its measure.
Remember praise by others won
  And pass it on with pleasure.
Remember every promise made
  And keep it to the letter.
Remember those who lend you aid
  And be a grateful debtor.

Remember all the happiness
  That comes your way in living.
Forget each worry and distress;
  Be hopeful and forgiving.
Remember good, remember truth,
  Remember Heaven's above you,
And you will find, through age and youth,
  True joys and hearts to love you.

Our sincere thanks to the author
whose address we were unable to locate.

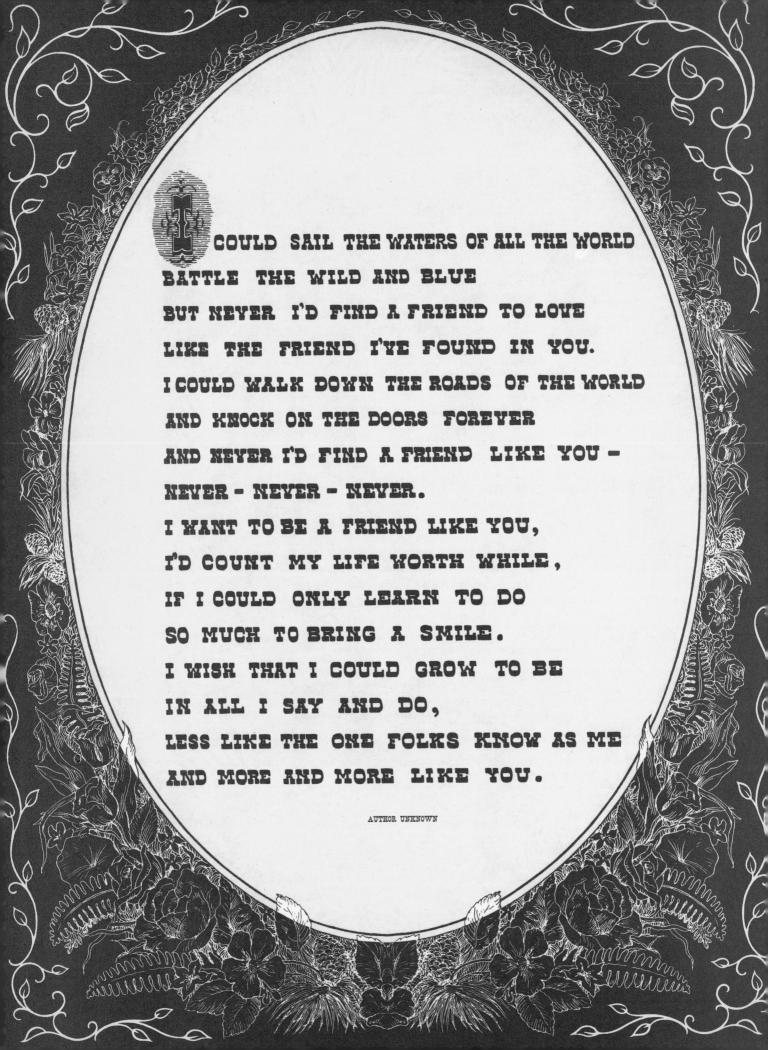

I COULD SAIL THE WATERS OF ALL THE WORLD
BATTLE THE WILD AND BLUE
BUT NEVER I'D FIND A FRIEND TO LOVE
LIKE THE FRIEND I'VE FOUND IN YOU.
I COULD WALK DOWN THE ROADS OF THE WORLD
AND KNOCK ON THE DOORS FOREVER
AND NEVER I'D FIND A FRIEND LIKE YOU -
NEVER - NEVER - NEVER.
I WANT TO BE A FRIEND LIKE YOU,
I'D COUNT MY LIFE WORTH WHILE,
IF I COULD ONLY LEARN TO DO
SO MUCH TO BRING A SMILE.
I WISH THAT I COULD GROW TO BE
IN ALL I SAY AND DO,
LESS LIKE THE ONE FOLKS KNOW AS ME
AND MORE AND MORE LIKE YOU.

AUTHOR UNKNOWN

MAKE NEW FRIENDS, BUT KEEP THE OLD;
THOSE ARE SILVER, THESE ARE GOLD.
NEW-MADE FRIENDSHIPS, LIKE NEW WINE,
AGE WILL MELLOW AND REFINE.
FRIENDSHIPS THAT HAVE STOOD THE TEST -
TIME AND CHANGE - ARE SURELY BEST;
BROW MAY WRINKLE, HAIR GROW GRAY,
FRIENDSHIP NEVER KNOWS DECAY.
FOR 'MID OLD FRIENDS, TRIED AND TRUE,
ONCE MORE WE OUR YOUTH RENEW.
BUT OLD FRIENDS, ALAS! MAY DIE,
NEW FRIENDS MUST THEIR PLACE SUPPLY.
CHERISH FRIENDSHIP IN YOUR BREAST -
NEW IS GOOD, BUT OLD IS BEST;
MAKE NEW FRIENDS, BUT KEEP THE OLD;
THOSE ARE SILVER, THESE ARE GOLD.

BY JOSEPH PARRY

Happiness

Priscilla Leonard

Happiness is like a crystal,
Fair and exquisite and clear,
Broken in a million pieces,
Shattered, scattered far and near.
Now and then along life's pathway,
Lo! some shining fragments fall;
But there are so many pieces
No one ever finds them all.

You may find a bit of beauty,
Or an honest share of wealth,
While another just beside you
Gathers honor, love or health.
Vain to choose or grasp unduly,
Broken is the perfect ball;
And there are so many pieces
No one ever finds them all.

Yet the wise, as on they journey,
Treasure every fragment clear,
Fit them as they may together,
Imagining the shattered sphere,
Learning ever to be thankful,
Though their share of it is small;
For it has so many pieces
No one ever finds them all.

Our sincere thanks to the author
whose address we were unable to locate.

YUNKSTER GAZETTE

Vol. 1, No. 1   HOMETOWN, U.S.A.

A Scoutmaster Saves the Day

A thrilling story of bravery and courage of a boy who finished a job, as told by star reporter, Walter MacPeek.

☙

BOYVILLE — For weeks the Troop had been engaged in expectant preparation for its Parents' Night program. Everything was in order. The walls were filled with displays — the Scouts with enthusiasm — and the tables with good things to eat.

The Toastmaster was well under way. The crowd sang with that respectably restrained enthusiasm which typified a Parents' Night program.

Then Jimmie Davis arose to give his oration. This was the moment to which he had looked forward for many weeks. As he arose he caught a glimpse of the beaming face of his mother and of his father's stolid assured countenance. He started with a great burst of enthusiasm. He waxed more eloquent, conscious that his hearers were paying a high tribute to him by their careful attention.

Then something happened. The world seemed to swim before him — he slowed down — faltered — stopped. His face flushed, his hands sought each other frantically and in desperation he looked helplessly toward his Scoutmaster.

And ever prepared, having heard that boyish masterpiece rehearsed again and again, the boy's leader supplied the missing words and the lad went on. But somehow it was different now. The masterpiece had been marred.

Jimmy paused again — and the Scoutmaster prompted him again. For the remaining two minutes the oration seemed more the Scoutmaster's than the boy's.

But Jimmie finished it. In the heart of the lad who sat down, knowing that he had failed, there was a heavy load. Chagrin was plainly written on the face of the boy's mother, and a twitch of the father's face indicated a pained consciousness of shame.

The audience applauded in a perfunctory way, sorry for and pitying the boy whom they thought had failed.

But the Scoutmaster was on his feet. His quiet eyes twinkled. All listened tensely for he did not talk loudly. What was he saying —

"I am more happy than any of you can possibly understand because of what has just happened. You have seen a boy make a glorious victory out of what might have been a miserable failure.

"Jimmie had his chance to quit. To have quit would have been easy. But to *finish the job* even in the face of two hundred people required the highest kind of bravery and courage I know.

"You may some day hear a better oratorical effect, but I am confident that you will never see a finer demonstration of the spirit of our Troop — than Jimmie has just given you — to play the game even under difficulties!"

The people thundered their applause now. Jimmie's mother sat straight and proud. The old look of assurance was back on the face of the boy's father. The entire group was enthusiastic again, and Jimmie, with a lump in his throat, said something to the friend beside him that sounded like, "Gee, if I can be that kind of a Scoutmaster some day."

WOULD YOU DIFFER?

"In the evening of a long toilsome life, if a man were obliged to solemnly declare what, without any exception, has been the most lovely thing which, on the surface of this earth, it has been his good fortune to witness — I conceive, without hesitation, he might reply, 'The mind of a young child.' "

I recently came across these words in a book written for children way back in 1838. And who would differ with the writer?

☙

Building Boys is Better Than Mending Men.

General Douglas MacArthur Describes Youth in His 75th Birthday Speech

★★★★★

Youth is not entirely a time of life — it is a state of mind. It is not wholly a matter of ripe cheeks, red lips or supple knees. It is a temper of the will, a quality of the imagination, a vigor of the emotions, a freshness of the deep springs of life. It means a temperamental predominance of courage over timidity, of an appetite for adventure over love of ease.

Nobody grows old by merely living a number of years. People grow old only by deserting their ideals. Years may wrinkle the skin, but to give up interest wrinkles the soul. Worry, doubt, self-distrust, fear and despair — these are the long, long years that bow the head and turn the growing spirit back to dust. Whatever your years, there is in every being's heart the love of wonder, the undaunted challenge of events, the unfailing child-like appetite for what next, and the joy and the game of life.

You are as young as your faith, as old as your doubt; as young as your self-confidence, as old as your fear; as young as your hope, as old as your despair. In the central place of every heart there is a recording chamber; so long as it receives messages of beauty, hope, cheer and courage, so long are you young. When the wires are all down and your heart is covered with the snow of pessimism and the ice of cynicism, then, and then only are you grown old.

MISTER MEAN-TO

Mr. Mean-To has a comrade, and his name is Didn't-Do; Have you ever chanced to meet them? Did they ever call on you? These two fellows live together in the house of Never-Win; And I'm told it is haunted by the ghost of —

Might-Have-Been.

John Carmody Reads Beautiful Story

*As told by our special
reporter, Michael Foster*

It's queer, the things you remember. When life has crumbled suddenly, and left you standing there, alone. It's not the big important things that you remember when you come to that: not the plans of years, not the love nor the hopes you've worked so hard for. It's the little things that you remember then: the little things you hadn't noticed at the time. The way a hand touched yours, and you too busy to notice; the hopeful little inflection of a voice you didn't really bother to listen to.

John Carmody found that out, staring through the living-room window at the cheerful Tuesday afternoon life of the street. He kept trying to think about the big important things, lost now — the years and the plans, and the hopes, and the love. But he couldn't quite get them focused sharply in his mind just now — not this afternoon.

They — those important things — were like a huge but nebulous background in his mind. All he could remember, now, was a queer little thing: nothing, really, if you stopped and thought about it in the light of the years and the plans and the — the great love. It was only something his little girl had said to him one evening, two — perhaps three weeks ago. Nothing, if you looked at it rationally — the sort of thing that kids are always saying.

But it was what he was remembering, now.

That particular night, he had brought home from the office a finished draft of the annual stockholders' report. Very important, it was. Things being as they were, it meant a great deal — to his future; to the future of his wife and his little girl. He sat down to re-read it before dinner. It had to be right; it meant so much.

And just as he turned a page, Marge, his little girl, came with a book under her arm. It was a green-covered book, with a fairy-tale picture pasted on it. And she said: "Look, Daddy." He glanced up and said: "Oh, fine. A new book, eh?"

"Yes, Daddy," she said. "Will you read me a story in it?" "No, dear. Not just now," he said.

Marge just stood there, and he read through a paragraph which told the stockholders about certain replacements in the machinery of the factory. And Marge's voice, with timid and hopeful little inflections, was saying:

"But Mummy said you probably would, Daddy."

He looked up over the top of the typescript. "I'm sorry," he answered. "Maybe Mummy will read it to you. I'm busy, dear."

"No," Marge said politely. "Mummy is much busier upstairs. Won't you read me just this one story? Look — it has a picture. See? Isn't it a *lovely* picture, Daddy?"

"Oh, yes. Beautiful," he said. "Now that picture has class, hasn't it? But I do have to work tonight. Some other time . . ."

After that, there was quite a long silence. Marge just stood there with the book open at the lovely picture. It was a long time before she said anything else. He read through two more pages explaining in full detail, as he had directed, the shift in markets over the past twelve months, the plans outlined by the sales department for meeting these problems which, after all, could safely be ascribed to local conditions, and the advertising program which after weeks of conferences had been devised to stabilize and even increase the demand for their products.

"But it *is* a lovely picture, Daddy. And the story looks *so* exciting," Marge said.

"I know," he said. "Ah . . . Mmmmm. Some other time. Run along, now."

"I'm sure you'd enjoy it, Daddy," Marge said. "Eh? Yes. I know I would. But later . . .

"Oh," Marge said. "Well, some other time then. Will you, Daddy, some other time?"

"Oh, of course," he said. "You bet."

But she didn't go away. She still stood there quietly, like a good child. And after a long time, she put the book down on the stool at his feet, and said: "Well, whenever you get ready, just read it to yourself. Only read it loud enough so I can hear too." "Sure," he said, "sure — later."

And that was what John Carmody was remembering — now, not the long plans of love and care for the years ahead. He was remembering the way a well-mannered child had touched his hand with timid little fingers, and said: "Just read it to yourself. Only read it loud enough so I can hear too."

And that was why, now, he put

(Continued on next page)

JOHN CARMODY (continued)

his hand on the book from the corner table, where they had piled some of Marge's playthings, picking them up from the floor where she had left them.

The book wasn't new anymore; and the green cover was dented and thumbed. He opened it to the *lovely* picture.

And reading that story, his lips moving stiffly with anguish to form the words, he didn't try to think anymore, as he should be thinking, about the important things: about his careful and shrewd and loving plans for the years to come; and for a little while he forgot, even, the horror and bitterness of his hate for the half-drunken driver who had careened down the street in a second-hand car — and who was now in jail on manslaughter charges.

He didn't even see his wife — white and silent — dressed to be with Marge for the last time, standing in the doorway, trying to make her voice say calmly, "I'm ready, dear. We must go."

Because John Carmody was reading:

"Once upon a time there was a little girl who lived in a woodcutter's hut, in the Black Forest. And she was so fair that the birds forgot their singing from the bough, looking at her. And there came a day when . . ."

He was reading it to himself. But loud enough for her to hear, too. Maybe.

©

ON TAKING BIG BITES
S. R. Knowlton

Once I learned a lesson,
And I'll pass it on to you,
So when you're at a party
You'll know what not to do.

I was eating chocolate cookies —
And of course 'twas not polite —
But they were so very good,
I took a great big bite.

Just then the hostess asked me,
"Do you want some ice cream, Joe?"
But I could only mumble,
And she thought that I said "No!"

©

Unknown Author Aptly Describes Boys

After a male baby has grown out of long clothes and triangles and has acquired pants, freckles, and so much dirt that relatives do not dare to kiss it between meals, it becomes a BOY. A boy is Nature's answer to that false belief that there is no such thing as perpetual motion. A boy can swim like a fish, run like a deer, climb like a squirrel, balk like a mule, bellow like a bull, eat like a pig, or act like a jackass, according to climatic conditions.

He is a piece of skin stretched over an appetite. A noise covered with smudges. He is called a tornado because he comes at the most unexpected times, hits the most unexpected places, and leaves everything a wreck behind him.

He is a growing animal of superlative promise, to be fed, watered, and kept warm; a joy forever, a periodic nuisance, the problem of our times, the hope of a nation.

Every boy born is evidence that God is not yet discouraged of man.

Were it not for boys, the newspapers would go unread and a thousand picture shows would go bankrupt. Boys are useful in running errands. A boy can easily do the family errands with the aid of five or six adults. The zest with which a boy does an errand is equaled only by the speed of a turtle on a July day.

The boy is a natural spectator. He watches parades, fires, fights, ball games, automobiles, boats, and airplanes with equal fervor, but will not watch the clock.

The man who invents a clock that will stand on its head and sing a song when it strikes will win the undying gratitude of millions of families whose boys are forever coming to lunch about supper time.

Boys faithfully imitate their dads in spite of all efforts to teach them good manners. A boy, if not washed too often and if kept in a cool, quiet place after each accident, will survive broken bones, hornets, swimming holes, fights, and nine helpings of pie.

When he grows up he'll trade puppy love, energy, warts, bashfulness, and a cast-iron stomach for a bay window, pride, ambition, pretense, a bald head, and will immediately begin to say that "boys aren't what they used to be in the good old days."

THE TOWN OF DON'T-YOU-WORRY
I. J. Bartlett

There's a town called Don't-You-Worry
On the banks of River Smile,
Where the Cheer-Up and Be-Happy
Blossom sweetly all the while.
Where the Never-Grumble flower
Blooms beside the fragrant Try,
And the Ne'er-Give-Up and Patience
Point their faces to the sky.

*In the valley of Contentment,
In the province of I-Will,
You will find this lovely city,
At the foot of No-Fret hill,
There are thoroughfares delightful
In this very charming town,
And on every hand are shade trees
Named the Very-Seldom-Frown.*

Rustic benches, quite enticing
You'll find scattered here and there;
And to each a vine is clinging
Called the Frequent-Earnest—Prayer.
Everybody there is happy,
And is singing all the while,
In the town of Don't-You-Worry
On the banks of River Smile.

©

Writer Clee Shupp Urges Secret Place For Every Child

Every child must have a secret place. A secret place where no adult can enter. A secret place to which a child can withdraw when his grown-ups have let him down with their unexplainable adult logic. The secret place will be there and he will be lost in the sheer joy of having something to which he can cling that will not be yanked away from him, something that will not fail him, that he doesn't have to understand, but is simply there waiting for him when he needs it.

The secret place can be almost anything or anywhere. Whatever it is it will be something that an adult wouldn't possibly waste valuable time on. It can be right in his own front yard, under a towering clump of lilacs that roof a hollowed-out place no adult can see. It can be the tall, sweet grass in the orchard, or under the lone tree left standing in the middle of the field to mark the rock pile. It can be most anywhere where a small child can sit and think and try to figure things out. There are so many, many things a child must try to figure out for himself and where better than a secret place apart from the grown-up world that demands so much and gives so little of understanding?

Secret places can be ever so small. A flat rock which upturned very gently reveals a mysterious doorway into the earth. Only a spider's hole . . . never mind! To the curious seeking of a child it is a wonderful secret to be carefully hidden from dull grown-up eyes. A wonderful secret to be rediscovered countless times. It can be a hollowed-out branch of a tree in which to cache polished stones, nutshells, and bits of blue glass. It can be a still pool in the tiny creek that struggles through the pasture field. A still pool where the child comes day after day hoping to find fish. For in a child's world can not anything happen?

A secret place can be a thing of grandeur. Just such a one was my secret place to which my sister Becky and I retreated when the grown-up world became too much for us to understand. (Secret places can be shared with someone very dear, of course, if they promise never, never to tell a single living soul, cross their heart and hope to die.) Our secret place was a huge, huge, huge tree which had been felled in some mysterious way across a ravine deep in the woods, much farther than we were allowed to go. It had fallen in such a way that its tremendous trunk spanned the ravine forming a bridge, and its branches rested at one side of the ravine forming smaller bridges. Oh it was a wondrous awesome sight! Each time we drew near the ravine within sight of our secret place we hesitated and gazed at it with fresh delight and wonder as if we had just then come upon it for the first time.

We climbed upon the trunk and carefully tight-rope-walked our way across to the other side and then back, daring to look down below us into the abyss of the ravine. Now that with years I have acquired the dull eyes of an adult, I know the ravine was quite small and the depth of no consequence, the tree merely an old tree that had grown tired of clinging to the ravine bank and had toppled over. But fortunately a child's eyes see what they want to see.

This was our secret place. Our Grand Canyon we called it. Somewhere we had heard of the Grand Canyon out west, but how could any canyon be more magnificent than this our own Grand Canyon? And when we found ourselves baffled by our grown-ups, we whispered the secret words, Grand Canyon, and ran breathlessly across the field into the woods. Somehow our world was always turned right side up again after a few minutes of enchanted lostness in our secret place.

How can children bound by city walls have a secret place? How can they find the mysterious abodes built under flat rocks, the place where the first violets come. How can they find the ledge under the cliff that is velveted with moss, the hidden spring that trickles from under a gnarled willow root and as suddenly loses itself into the ground. How can a child know the fullest joy of childhood without once having a secret place all his own that he had discovered all alone and no one else in all the whole wide world knows about unless he cares to tell them?

In the world of grown-ups is there a secret place? ©

BUILDERS — *Hattie Vose Hall*

A Builder builded a temple,
He wrought it with grace and skill;
Pillars and groins and arches
All fashioned to work his will.
Men said, as they saw its beauty,
"It shall never know decay;
Great is thy skill, O Builder!
Thy fame shall endure for aye."

A Teacher builded a temple
With loving and infinite care,
Planning each arch with patience,
Laying each stone with prayer.
None praised her unceasing efforts,
None knew of her wondrous plan,
For the temple the Teacher builded
Was unseen by the eyes of man.

Gone is the Builder's temple,
Crumbled into the dust;
Low lies each stately pillar,
Food for consuming rust,
But the temple the Teacher builded
Will last while the ages roll,
For that beautiful unseen temple
Was a child's immortal soul.

©

*Our sincere appreciation to
the author whose address we
were unable to locate.*

Childhood Days Most Important To Nation's Future

Mr. George Matthew Adams, the world famous author and lecturer, said on the subject—

"Every child is interesting because its eyes open to a world never dreamed about. Looking upon each one is like viewing the unfolding of a mystery. There are no days so filled with wonder and curiosity as those of childhood.

"It is while the brain is plastic that substantial paths can work their way and give a foundation for the life that is to follow. Early impressions do not easily fade out. Creating interest in the child mind is the first step to its growth of mind and character. Each new interest is a stimulant to other ones, resulting in a healthy imagination.

"Every possible interest should be thrown in a child's way. Originality should be encouraged, no matter how crude the attempts. And inclinations should always be endorsed. A child is ever conscious of its early discoveries and tendencies, and great care should be taken never to discourage a happy effort by a child.

"Nothing in this world is so substantial a foundation for a great nation as a well regulated and happy home, with normal children in it. Stimulate those young minds with healthy toys and instructive books and you will have little or no fear as to their natural development a little later on. Nothing stays by a child like a taste for good books.

"It is in the home that the earliest tendencies of a child are shown, and by right guidance principles are established that become the real foundation stones to after life character and its happy success as well. Every wholesome influence should surround every child in its own home and it won't wish to wander from it.

Picture of happy childhood days.

"The citadel of a nation is its homes. Within them are the seeds of its greatness, and the assurance of its long and useful life. There is no influence so potent as that which contacts the child in its home. Everything should be done to make that home attractive and inviting so that its memory may long linger in the mind.

"Childhood's days are all too short. They pass so quickly. An unhappy childhood is a tragic thing. A community's greatest investment is that which it has in its youth. It cannot do too much to develop healthy sports, good schools, and libraries. They all pay dividends in good citizenship."

God's Children—James J. Metcalfe

Although God loves the whole wide world . . . And blesses every part . . . I think He has a special place . . . For children in His heart . . . I think He cherishes their smiles . . . Their eagerness and mirth . . . And their appreciation of . . . The wonders of His earth . . . I think He listens closely to . . . Whatever words they say . . . I think He follows them to school . . . And watches them at play . . . And when they go to bed at night . . . He probably is there . . . To see that they have happy dreams . . . Beneath their tousled hair . . . All children in a special way . . . Belong to God above . . . And I am sure He favors them . . . With everlasting love.

Angelo Patri Admonishes All Parents To Praise Something in Each Child Every Day.

Praise, wisely bestowed, is a powerful stimulant to the growth and development of children. Their longing for approval is instinctive and compelling and they never cease striving to win it.

In their efforts to grow up and become like the admired adults children make mistakes. That is the time for teachers and parents to take heed to what they say and do, time to stop and endeavor to see through the behavior to the need that prompted it.

Bruno, aged fifteen, was a thorn in the side of his family. Father spoke severely about his failings in school and at home; Mother chided him for bad manners and untidiness; little brother complained loudly of his rough treatment. Bruno's ways remained unchanged while his gloom deepened and his temper heightened.

One morning after an unusually disturbing session his mother said, "It does seem to me that for once, just once, you might behave like a human being. You're nothing but a nuisance about the house."

Granny halted on her way to the kitchen and beaming over her specs at the glowering Bruno said, "Lay off that boy. He's the only one in the house who can build a decent fire, and I'd have you know that takes brains and some strength. He'll be a man to be proud of some day." Bruno grew red about the ears and slid out of the room. "Mark me, Mary. You'd better have a good word for that boy or you'll lose him," said Granny, and went her benevolent way.

Mother was quick to take the hint and from that day on Bruno's life was easier. His growth made him clumsy, uncertain and afraid, and sharp criticism added to his unfitness. An understanding word, a bit

Continued on next page

PRAISE   (continued)

of praise warmed his spirit and lifted the weight off his mind. His work improved, his attitudes changed and because he was happier he was easier to help.

Praise need not be direct and personal to affect the lives and characters of children. They are quick to note the people and things which those they love and admire choose as their particular treasure. "I'll take what you take," is the child's way of keeping hold on approval, of making sure of that feeling of friendly togetherness that means so much to him.

Then praise good deeds. Praise good men. Praise something in each child every day. If there is only one good line in his drawings, praise that. If there is one good phrase, even one colorful word in his compositions, praise that. If there is nothing else that in honesty you can praise, then praise his eyes. They are always beautiful and especially so when lighted by affectionate understanding of your approval.

Copyrighted and used by special permission of Redbook Magazine.

𝔚𝔥𝔢𝔫 𝔞 𝔉𝔞𝔱𝔥𝔢𝔯 𝔓𝔯𝔞𝔶𝔰

Build me a son, oh Lord, who will be strong enough to know when he is weak and brave enough to face himself when he is afraid. One who will be proud and unbending in defeat, but humble and gentle in victory.

A son whose wishbone will not be where his backbone should be; a son who will know, that to know himself, is the foundation stone of all true knowledge.

Rear him, I pray, not in the path of ease and comfort, but under the stress and spur of difficulties and challenges. Here let him learn to stand up in the storm; here let him learn compassion for those who fall.

Build me a son whose heart will be clean, whose goal will be high. A son who will master himself, before he seeks to master other men. One who will learn to laugh, but never forget how to weep. One who will reach far into the future, yet never forget the past.

And after all these are his, add I pray, enough of a sense of humor so that he may always be serious yet never take himself too seriously; a touch of humility, so that he may always remember the simplicity of true greatness; the open mind of true wisdom; the meekness of true strength.

Then, I, his father, will dare in the sacred recesses of my own heart to whisper: "I have not lived in vain."

CHILDREN AND CHANCE   —   *by Richard L. Evans*

On Sunday morning, January 11, 1948, this inspiring address by Richard L. Evans was heard over Radio Station KSL and CBS, from the Tabernacle, Temple Square, Salt Lake City, Utah. We are happy to be privileged to bring it to our readers at this time.

Almost everyone, it would seem, has his own ideas on the care and counsel of children. For some, the process does not mean much more than providing the physical necessities — if that. For others, it means minutely prescribing everything. Both are questionable extremes. Perhaps no one can say with finality just how far we should go in either direction, because children differ, and so do parents, and so do circumstances.

But this it would surely be safe to say: that the shaping of the thoughts and characters and lives of children should not be left too much to chance. It isn't possible for us to insulate them from all unlooked-for influences, nor, perhaps, would it always be desirable. But if we leave their lives too exposed, we issue an open invitation to chance.

And what comes in at the open door may not be what it should be. To be sure, many things are going to come into their lives anyway that neither we nor they can control. But where we can counsel and safeguard and wisely control, we have an obligation to do so. Few things that matter much can be safely left to chance.

The farmer's crops, for example, are subject to many uncertainties. But a wise farmer doesn't leave them at the mercy of chance if he can avoid it. He doesn't let pests and parasites and other undesirable elements make inroads if he can keep them out. And if he does leave too much to chance, he may have a crop of weeds. And any business that is left to chance is likely soon to become insolvent.

And there is no more important business before us, none with more far-reaching consequences to our own happiness and to the happiness of generations to come, than the guiding and the safeguarding of our children.

It is written that there was a man who cared for his flocks and his fields, and for his stocks and his bonds with great care, but who didn't know so much about where his children went or what they saw or what they heard or whom they were with. It is not written, however, that he was a wise man.

We have an obligation to be ever alert to all that pertains to our children. And the less of this we leave to chance, the more we fill their lives with the right things, the less room there will be for the wrong things.   ©

*From AT THIS SAME HOUR by Richard L. Evans.
Used by permission of Harper & Brothers.*

Somewhere Today is an Unknown Teacher and An Unknown Boy Who Will Change the World

Fifteen years ago a short article of faith and inspiration written by Joy Elmer Morgan was featured in the National Education Journal. We are happy to be privileged to again present this to our readers—

Somewhere in a schoolroom today under the care of an unknown teacher is a child who in his own time, grown to maturity, will lead the world away from war and toward peace.

The affection planted in that child's life by wise guidance; the sense of right values with which he is constantly surrounded; the integrity and initiative that are fostered in his unfolding life will come to fruition in a mighty service to the human race.

It is a wise providence that no one can tell which of the millions of babies born in our country each year is to be this savior of tomorrow. We are done with king-children and their pampered training to maintain a class system. We want the children of the people, of all the people — rich and poor of every race and creed — to have their chance.

And when thru honest growth, proved merit, and wise leadership the pilots of tomorrow take their places at the helm, we want them to be surrounded and supported by their fellows likewise schooled in the simple and abiding principles of democracy.

With this purpose and in this faith, the teachers of America carry on. This faith was good enough for the founding fathers who launched this ship of state in even more troubled seas than we now face. This faith has been good enough for the teachers and prophets of all ages who have understood the power of human aspiration and growth.

It is the faith of Jesus — the Golden Rule and the brotherhood of man. It is the faith that for 1900 years has held aloft thru good times and bad the torch of eternal truth. We renew our faith in this destiny of the individual human soul lifted by true teaching thru the leavening power of God's grace to nobility and wisdom.

This faith of the teacher — your faith and mine as we look into the eager faces of youth — is the hope of tomorrow, a hope that cannot fail. It is bigger than all the fears and partisanships of our time. Let us renew and deepen our faith.

Two Prayers

Last night my little boy
  confessed to me
Some childish wrong;
And kneeling at my knee,
He prayed with tears —
"Dear God, make me a man
Like daddy — wise and strong;
I know You can."

Then while he slept
I knelt beside his bed,
Confessed my sins,
And prayed with low-bowed
  head,
"Oh God, make me a child
Like my child here —
Pure, guileless,
Trusting Thee with faith
  sincere."

From a very old scrapbook. Our sincere thanks to the author, Andrew Gillies, whose address we have been unable to locate.

If we work on marble, it will perish; if we work upon brass, time will efface it; if we rear temples, they will crumble into dust; but if we work upon immortal souls, if we imbue them with principles, with the just fear of the Creator and love of fellow men, we engrave on those tablets something which will brighten all eternity.

Daniel Webster

★

Never tell a young person that something can not be done. God may have been waiting for centuries for somebody ignorant enough of the impossibility to do that thing.

Dr. J. A. Holmes

★

The kind of a world we live in tomorrow depends—not partially— but entirely upon the type and quality of the education of our children today.

Martin Vanbee

IT TAKES SO LITTLE

Fathers who never get to know their sons miss one of life's most precious experiences, one they can ill afford to lose. They go lonely all their days, and their boys go through life with an aching emptiness that nothing ever quite fills. Even the healing touch of Time fails to comfort the longing of a child for his father. "If Father had only —"

A father needs the renewal of youth that keeping step with his son's growth must inevitably bring. It is simple enough. All that is needed is a day-by-day sharing, listening, helping — a father's seasoned soul lending power to his son's budding growth through shared experiences that give the boy a feeling of security in his father's sustaining love.

There are many occasions when a father can play special providence to his boy and knit himself still closer in affection. When the first pair of real boy's pants, that symbol of his masculinity so anxiously awaited, are to be bought, Father himself takes the boy, clinging to a finger, to the men's shop. He helps select the color and the style; he counts the pockets and admires the fit. The event becomes a high holiday, and Father its particular patron saint.

The next occasion comes as a surprise. One evening Father says with careful casualness: "I got something for you today. Just get that little package you will find in my overcoat pocket. See if you like it."

A scrambling rush, an instant of silence, then a shout of delight. "For me? Father! how ever did you know I wanted a knife?" Proudly he strokes its single blade. Butter would give it trouble; but to him it is a blade of Damascus. It is the first of a long line, but none other, however smart its gadgetry, will ever compare with this. And it was Father who thought of it.

When the first "longies" are

Continued on next page

IT TAKES SO LITTLE (cont.)

to be bought, of course Father goes along. If he remembers and misses the little hand clinging to his finger, he shows no sign of it, but enthusiastically enters into the selection of this all-important suit. He tries to be very matter-of-fact when the self-conscious young man stands before him asking: "Think this blue is all right on me?" Father approves the color, praises the fit and the style. He likes it all immensely, and two men walk out of the shop and up the street, shoulder to shoulder, swinging along in time. 'Tis a perfect day.

By and by Father takes the boy to college and leaves him there, knowing that he has said good-by to the boy that he has walked beside for eighteen years or so. But he goes home smiling, knowing well that when the young man returns, he will come as one nearer than a friend, closer than a brother. He will be a son.

It takes so little, to make all the difference. If fathers only knew —

This beautiful article by Angelo Patri was featured in the June 1936 issue of the Redbook Magazine. Reprinted here by special permission. Copyright, 1936.

Be Patient With the Boys

I have a profound respect for a boy. His life is big with possibilities.

He may make or unmake kings, change boundary lines between states, write books that will mold characters, or invent machines that will revolutionize the commerce of the world.

Every man was once a boy. I trust I shall not be contradicted; it is really so.

Very distinctly and vividly I remember a slim, freckled boy, who was born in the "Patch," and used to pick up coal along the railroad tracks in Buffalo. A few months ago I had a motion to make before the Supreme Court, and the boy from the "Patch" was the judge who wrote the opinion granting my petition.

Yesterday I rode horseback past a field where a boy was plowing. The lad's hair stuck out through the top of his hat; his form was bony and awkward; one suspender held his trousers in place; his bare legs and arms were brown and sunburned and briar scarred.

He swung his horses around just as I passed by, and from under the flapping brim of his hat he cast a quick glance out of the dark, half-bashful eyes and modestly returned my salute. His back turned, I took off my hat and sent a God-bless-you down the furrow after him. Who knows? — I may go to that boy to borrow money, or to hear him preach, or to beg him to defend me in a lawsuit; or he may stand with pulse unhastened, bare of arm, in white apron, ready to do his duty, while the cone is placed over my face, and Night and Death come creeping into my veins.

Be patient with the boys — you are dealing with soulstuff.

Destiny awaits just around the corner. Be patient with the boys.

Written a generation ago by Elbert Hubbard.
Copyrighted.
Used by permission Elbert Hubbard II.

Never fear spoiling children by making them too happy. Happiness is the atmosphere in which all good affections grow.

Thomas Bray

*

The fairest flower in the garden of creation is a young mind, offering and unfolding itself to the influence of divine wisdom, as the heliotrope turns its sweet blossom to the sun.

Joseph Russel Smith

*

If thou canst believe, all things are possible to him that believeth.

Mark 9:23

*

Children need models more than they need critics.

Joseph Joubert (1842)

*

Train up a child in the way he should go: and when he is grown he will not depart from it.

Proverbs 22:6

*

It's what we learn after we think we know it all that counts.

Abe Martin

PITTYPAT and TIPPYTOE
EUGENE FIELD

All day long they come and go—
Pittypat and Tippytoe;
Footprints up and down the hall,
Playthings scattered on the floor,
Finger-marks along the wall,
Tell-tale smudges on the door—
By these presents you shall know
Pittypat and Tippytoe.

How they riot at their play!
And a dozen times a day
In they troop, demanding bread—
Only buttered bread will do,
And that butter must be spread
Inches thick with sugar too!
And I never can say, "No,
Pittypat and Tippytoe!"

Sometimes there are griefs to soothe,
Sometimes ruffled brows to smooth;
For (I much regret to say)
Tippytoe and Pittypat
Sometimes interrupt their play
With an internecine spat;
Fie, for shame! to quarrel so—
Pittypat and Tippytoe!

Oh, the thousand worrying things
Every day recurrent brings!
Hands to scrub and hair to brush,
Search for playthings gone amiss,
Many a wee complaint to hush,
Many a little bump to kiss;
Life seems one vain, fleeting show
To Pittypat and Tippytoe!

And when day is at an end,
There are little duds to mend:
Little frocks are strangely torn,
Little shoes great holes reveal,
Little hose, but one day worn,
Rudely yawn at toe and heel!
Who but you could work such woe,
Pittypat and Tippytoe?

But when comes this thought to me:
"Some there are that childless be,"
Stealing to their little beds,
With a love I cannot speak,
Tenderly I stroke their heads—
Fondly kiss each velvet cheek.
God help those who do not know
A Pittypat and Tippytoe!

On the floor and down the hall,
Rudely smutched upon the wall,
There are proofs in every kind
Of the havoc they have wrought,
And upon my heart you'd find
Just such trade-marks, if you sought;
Oh, how glad I am 'tis so,
Pittypat and Tippytoe!

Reprinted from POEMS OF CHILDHOOD by Eugene Field; used by permission of the publishers, Charles Scribner's Sons.

Sometimes, looking deep into the eyes of a child, you are conscious of meeting a glance full of wisdom. The child has known nothing yet but love and beauty — all this piled-up world knowledge you have acquired is unguessed at by him. And yet you meet this wonderful look which tells you in a moment more than all the years of experience have seemed to teach.

Hildegarde Hawthorne

Keep Your Dreams

Donald J. O'Connor

Not long ago there came the urge
To visit scenes of yore,
I felt my pulse begin to surge
With such a trip in store.
I'd see again the little school
And wander o'er the hill,
Until I reached the swimmin' pool
Behind the creaking mill.

The courthouse clock, the village square,
The park on Pleasant Street,
I felt would all be waiting there
To welcome friendly feet.
The folks would stop to mingle,
Most of them old pals of mine,
And I sensed a happy tingle
For the sake of Auld Lang Syne.

If you've ever gone as I did,
To the haunts of long ago,
Where in childhood you abided,
Then I'm certain you must know —
What a heartsick feeling lingers,
When you realize the change
That the years with tireless fingers
Bend their efforts to arrange.

I beheld with deep emotion
Buildings smart and up-to-date,
And I quickly lost the notion
That old-fashioned things will wait;
Just the swimmin' pool had lasted
And I watched its silent flow,
As each dream I had was blasted
Of the town I used to know.

Even friends shook hands discreetly
And 'twas then I realized,
Time had snapped the link completely
To the things we once had prized.
Had I known what lay in waiting
I'd have compromised with fact,
And be still anticipating —
With my happy dreams intact.

From an old scrapbook.
Our sincere thanks to the author
whose address we could not locate.

Friendship is a chain of God . . . Shaped in God's all perfect mold . . . Each link a smile, a laugh, a tear . . . A grip of the hand, a word of cheer . . . Steadfast as the ages roll . . . Binding closer soul to soul . . . No matter how far or heavy the load . . . Sweet is the journey on friendship's road.

Author Unknown

*

It's the giving and doing for somebody else . . . On that, all life's splendor depends . . . And the joys of this life, when you sum them all up . . . Are found in the making of friends.

Author Unknown

*

Give me a few friends who will love me for what I am, or am not, and keep ever burning before my wandering steps the kindly light of hope. And though age and infirmity overtake me, and I come not in sight of the castle of my dreams; teach me still to be thankful for life and time's old memories that are good and sweet. And may the evening twilight find me gentle still.

Author Unknown

*

When good friends walk beside us . . . On the trails that we must keep . . . Our burdens seem less heavy . . . And the hills are not so steep . . . The weary miles pass swiftly . . . Taken in a joyous stride . . . And all the world seems brighter . . . When friends walk by our side.

Author Unknown

*

This Was Christmas

Jessy Mae Coker

Rolling hills and pigmy canyons knee-deep in
soft, fluffy snow. Nights radiant with pale
light . . . sleigh rides . . . bells dancing on crisp,
quiet air!

*Weeks of dashing in after frosty hikes from
school to smell the sweet, spicy fragrance of
Mother's Christmas cookies . . . Dad's mysterious
trips to town to bring in those wonderful rustly
packages he hid in the closet!*

Sunday afternoon jaunts to the woods to pick
mistletoe, bittersweet, and cedar boughs to
decorate the parlor, or chinaberry pods to
make beads for a friend.

*Carefully saving pennies for that very special
gift . . . lingering hours along counters overflowing with the magic spoils of Christmas . . . the
heart-twisting decision between the gaudy
brooch, or the warm gloves Mother needed . . .
long, hungry looks at those beautiful doll
creatures with real hair!*

"Stringing night" . . . the tantalizing aroma of
Mother's fresh popped corn, which couldn't be
eaten until enough was strung for the tree . . .
singing carols while hanging ornaments on the
tree, mistletoe on chandeliers, bells on the
doors . . . heaping bowls of nuts, peppermint
sticks, twisted candy, big, round oranges,
shiny red apples . . . cracking "nigger-toes" on
a flat-iron!

*Then, Christmas Eve . . . early supper (but who
could eat?) . . . that delightful bedlam of dressing
for the Christmas program . . . shining faces,*

combed-down hair, and away we went, singing and chattering through crisp, clear night to the little country Church!

Ah, that giant Christmas tree, shimmering with stars, glittering tinsel, multicolored lights . . . dolls and toys bulging from every sprig . . . grownup songs and childish speeches . . . that breathless wait for my turn to recite!

At last! Santa with endless bags of treats and toys . . . that soul-crushing moment when he gives the real-hair doll to Susan across the aisle . . . "Adeste Fideles" and the greeting of friends . . . then home again to hang up stockings and rush to bed to sleep nervously the expectant night away!

Merry Christmas! At six in the morning . . . that tumbling race down the stairs . . . a real-hair doll (prettier than Susan's) sticking a head out of a stocking . . . eggnog, as only Dad could make it, for Christmas breakfast (but who could eat?) . . . again to church, this time to sing hymns and pray!

Finally, the famous Christmas feast . . . turkey with chestnut stuffing . . . candied yams . . . cranberry sauce . . . Grandma's fruit cake (made the year before) . . . and mince pie (and who couldn't eat?)

No school . . . a whole week to play with Santa's treasures . . . trips through drifting snow to Grandma's house . . . bobsleds and ice skating . . . family reunions . . . the awesome, thrilling, spellbinding tones of majestic chimes tolling "Silent Night"!

All this, and much, much more meant "Merry Christmas" when I was young!

Since it has been my lot to find . . . At every
parting of the road . . . The helping hand of
comrade kind . . . To help me with my heavy
load . . . And since I have no gold to give
. . . And love alone must make amends . . .
My humble prayer is, while I live . . .
"God make me worthy of my friends."

Author Unknown

*

We get the sweetest comfort . . . When we
wear the oldest shoe . . . We love the old
friends better . . . Than we'll ever love the new
. . . Old songs are more appealing . . . To the
wearied heart — and so . . . We find the sweetest music . . . In the tunes of long ago . . .
There's a kind of mellow sweetness . . . In a
good thing growing old . . . Each year that
rolls around it . . . Leaves an added touch
of gold.

Author Unknown

*

Tomorrow is not promised us . . . So let us
take today . . . And make the very most of it
. . . The once we pass this way . . . Just speak
aloud the kindly thought . . . And do the
kindly deed . . . And try to see and understand . . . Some fellow creature's need . . .
Tomorrow is not promised us . . . Nor any
other day . . . So let us make the most of it
. . . The once we pass this way.

Louise Mae Hogan ©

*

A friend is a present you give yourself.

Robert Louis Stevenson

*

When Winter Comes

Mrs. R. L. Peifer

Now let the winds of winter howl;
The snow heap high, in drifts,
The earth is white; the skies
   are gray
But sweet spring will come back
   some day
Bringing her priceless gifts.

We may be snow bound days and weeks,
Shut off from all our friends,
Jack Frost may paint our windows white
But stars will still be big and bright—
   And winter always ends!

Blizzards may roar, and streams
   be choked
With ice, but never mind
Beguile the dreary days away,
When winter comes, with work
   and play—
     Spring can't be far behind!

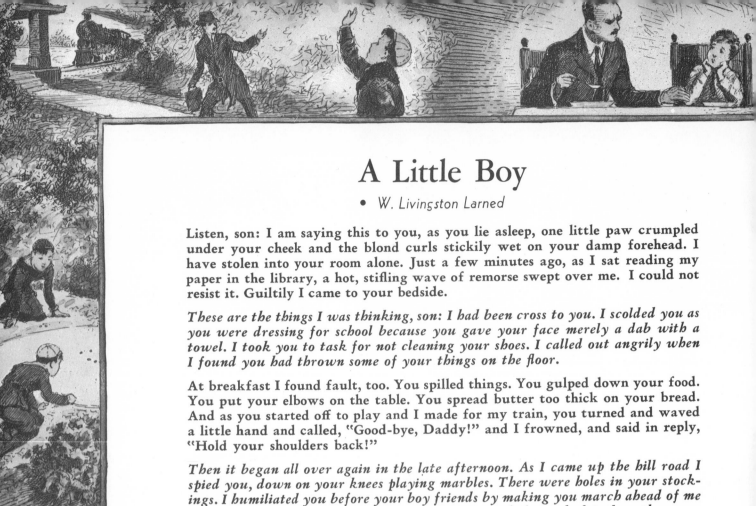

A Little Boy

• W. Livingston Larned

Listen, son: I am saying this to you, as you lie asleep, one little paw crumpled under your cheek and the blond curls stickily wet on your damp forehead. I have stolen into your room alone. Just a few minutes ago, as I sat reading my paper in the library, a hot, stifling wave of remorse swept over me. I could not resist it. Guiltily I came to your bedside.

These are the things I was thinking, son: I had been cross to you. I scolded you as you were dressing for school because you gave your face merely a dab with a towel. I took you to task for not cleaning your shoes. I called out angrily when I found you had thrown some of your things on the floor.

At breakfast I found fault, too. You spilled things. You gulped down your food. You put your elbows on the table. You spread butter too thick on your bread. And as you started off to play and I made for my train, you turned and waved a little hand and called, "Good-bye, Daddy!" and I frowned, and said in reply, "Hold your shoulders back!"

Then it began all over again in the late afternoon. As I came up the hill road I spied you, down on your knees playing marbles. There were holes in your stockings. I humiliated you before your boy friends by making you march ahead of me back to the house. Stockings were expensive—and if you had to buy them you would be more careful! Imagine that, son, from a father! It was such a stupid, silly logic.

Do you remember, later, when I was reading in the library, how you came in, softly, timidly, with a sort of hurt, hunted look in your eyes? When I glanced up over my paper, impatient at the interruption, you hesitated at the door.

"What is it that you want?" I snapped.

You said nothing, but ran across, in one tempestuous plunge, and threw your arms around my neck and kissed me, again and again, and your small arms tightened with affection that God had set blooming in your heart and which even neglect could not wither. And then you were gone, pattering up the stairs.

Well, son, it was shortly afterwards that my paper slipped from my hands and a terrible, sickening fear came over me. Suddenly I saw myself as I really was, in all my horrible selfishness, and I felt sick at heart.

What had habit been doing to me? The habit of complaining, of finding fault, of reprimanding—all of these were my rewards to you for being a boy. It was not that I did not love you; it was that I expected so much of youth. I was measuring you by the yardstick of my own years.

And there was so much that was good, and fine, and true in your character. You did not deserve my treatment of you, son. The little heart of you was as big as the dawn itself over the wide hills. All this was shown by your spontaneous impulse to rush in and kiss me good night. Nothing else matters tonight, son. I have come to your bedside in the darkness, and I have knelt here, choking with emotion, and so ashamed!

It is a feeble atonement, I know you would not understand these things if I told them to you during your waking hours, yet I must say what I am saying. I must burn sacrificial fires, here in your bedroom, and make free confession.

And I have prayed God to strengthen me in my new resolve. Tomorrow I will be a real daddy. I will chum with you, and suffer when you suffer and laugh when you laugh. I will bite my tongue when impatient words come. I will keep saying, as if it were a ritual: "He is nothing but a boy—a little boy!"

I am afraid I have visualized you as a man. Yet as I see you now, son, crumpled and weary in your cot, I see that you are still a baby. Yesterday you were in your mother's arms, your head on her shoulder. I have asked too much!

Dear boy! Dear little son! A penitent kneels at your infant shrine, here in the moonlight. I kiss the little fingers, and the damp forehead, and the yellow curls; and, if it were not for waking you, I would snatch you up and crush you to my breast.

Tears came, and heartache, and remorse, and—I think—a greater, deeper love, when you ran through the library door and wanted to kiss me!

Our sincere thanks to the author whose present address we could not locate — and for his personal permission granted our editor several years ago.

A Candle in the Night

Mary Stoner Wine

So very many people
Are like a candle in the night.
Their gentle noiseless beauty
Is like a steady burning light.

Though they be short and tiny
Or shapely tapers tall and fair,
Around them beams a radiance
That brightens life and steals our care.

They do not sense the darkness
Because their self-effacing glow
Encircles them with beauty
That shines alike on friend or foe.

And so I watch the candles
That banish darkness in the night,
Though they be short and tiny
Or tapers tall with flames of light.

The Philosopher

I'm not much on philosophy, I don't know all the creeds; I don't know what's inside the books my next door neighbor reads. I haven't studied ancient tongues, my English isn't good; I know I've said a lot of things that a scholar never would. But this is my experience, and so I'll pass it on; the time to be a friend to man is when he's needing one.

I don't discuss religion, much — I wouldn't if I could; I know I hate to draw a line between what's bad and good. I've had to plod along through life, and learn from other men, and so I've done a lot of things I'll never do again. But then, I found along the way, the time to be a friend is when a fellow's needin' all the help that you can lend.

I'm not much on philosophy, the books I never read; I've had to get the things I know from life that's hard indeed. I've never seen a winter through but I've had to stand alone, or seen some man without the means, and forced to make a loan. So if you have a cheer to give, or extra strength to lend—go out and help the man along who really needs a friend.

Our sincere thanks to the unknown author.

The Message of Christmas

Lucile Coleman

Christmas! What does it mean to you
And what does it mean to me?
Tinsel? Balls of red and blue
Glittering on a tree?
Mistletoe, candy canes, eggnogg,
The hanging of stockings for toys;
The glow of the Yuletide log;
Happy voices of girls and boys.
Christmas brings carols and holly
And bright cornucopias to fill,
A Santa Claus generous and jolly
With a bundle of love and good will.

Christmas means all these and more:
Three Magi that first Christmas night,
Who humbly knelt to adore
An Infant adorned with a bright
Golden halo around His small head,
Symbolizing Divine Origin;
A glorious star which had led
The three wise men to one little inn,
With their treasures of myrrh, frankincense,
With their love and devout worshiping;
To hail Mary with true reverence;
To give thanks for their newly born King.

Peace on earth and good will to men,
Welcomed with this Scriptural scene,
Brings Christmas to us, as did then
The birth of the Nazarene.

Father and Son

Edgar A. Guest

Be more than his dad,
    be a chum to the lad;
Be a part of his life,
    every hour of the day;
Find time to talk with him,
    take time to walk with him,
Share in his studies
    and share in his play;
Take him to places,
    to ball games and races,
Teach him the things that
    you want him to know;
Don't live apart from him,
    don't keep your heart from him,
Be his best comrade,
    he's needing you so!

Never neglect him,
    though young, still respect him,
Hear his opinions,
    with patience and pride;
Show him his error,
    but be not a terror,
Grim-visaged and fearful,
    when he's at your side.
Know all his playmates,
    it's easy to learn to;
Be such a father
    that when troubles gather
You'll be the first one
    for counsel, he'll turn to.

You can inspire him
    with courage, and fire him
Hot with ambition
    for deeds that are good;
He'll not betray you
    nor illy repay you,
If you have taught him
    the things that you should.
Father and son must
    in all things be one —
Partners in trouble
    and comrades in joy.
More than a dad
    was the best pal you had;
Be such a chum
    as you knew, to your boy.

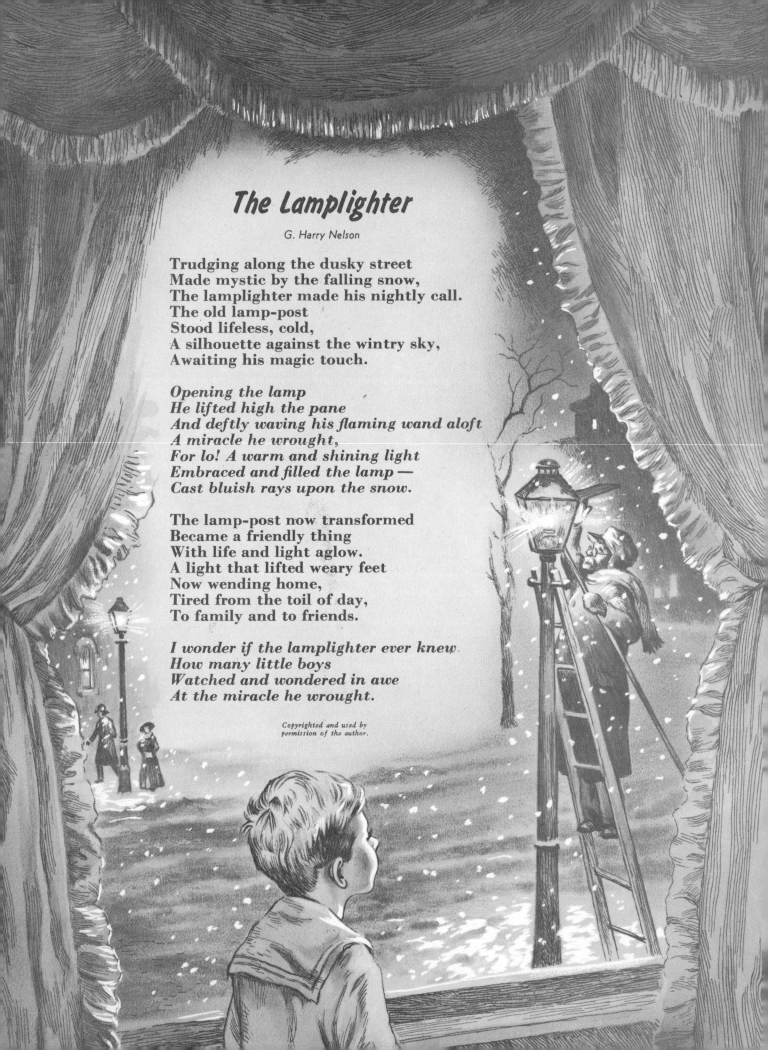

The Lamplighter

G. Harry Nelson

Trudging along the dusky street
Made mystic by the falling snow,
The lamplighter made his nightly call.
The old lamp-post
Stood lifeless, cold,
A silhouette against the wintry sky,
Awaiting his magic touch.

Opening the lamp
He lifted high the pane
And deftly waving his flaming wand aloft
A miracle he wrought,
For lo! A warm and shining light
Embraced and filled the lamp —
Cast bluish rays upon the snow.

The lamp-post now transformed
Became a friendly thing
With life and light aglow.
A light that lifted weary feet
Now wending home,
Tired from the toil of day,
To family and to friends.

I wonder if the lamplighter ever knew
How many little boys
Watched and wondered in awe
At the miracle he wrought.

From the editor's SCRAP BOOK

Today is the day I have been looking for. All my life has been spent in preparation for it. Yesterday and tomorrow are faraway nothings—the one a faint memory, the other a vague promise. But this is my day. It offers all that God has to give, and I'm a laggard or a coward if I fail to make the most of it.

Anonymous

Life isn't long a mother's song . . . And then another's smile . . . Then romping feet, and then the sweet . . . Remembrances awhile . . . From gold to gray, from dawn to day . . . And then the twilight hours . . . Life is too brief to hunt for grief . . . For thorns among the flowers.

If hurt today by what men say . . . If wounded by a friend . . . Oh, let tonight set all things right . . . Let trouble have an end . . . Life is too short to let report . . . Or rumor long annoy . . . Today has had so much so glad . . . We need it all for joy.

God's world, God's word, His breeze, His bird . . . No hand can rob you of . . . Wrong comes too late for hearts to hate . . . There is so much to love . . . Life isn't long, just time for song . . . And love, and things sublime . . . Be not concerned with thoughts that burned . . . Good friends, there isn't time.

Author Unknown

There is a destiny that makes us brothers . . . None goes his way alone . . . All that we send into the lives of others . . . Comes back into our own . . . I care not what his temples or his creeds . . . One thing holds firm and fast . . . That into his fateful heap of days and deeds . . . The soul of man is cast.

Edwin Markham

There is only one thing for us to do, and that is to do our level best right where we are, every day of our lives; to use our best judgments, and then to trust the rest to that Power which holds the focus of the universe in His hands and which doeth all things well.

O. S. Marden

O give me the joy of living . . . And some glorious work to do . . . A spirit of thanksgiving . . . With loyal heart and true . . . Some pathway to make brighter . . . Where tired feet now stray . . . Some burden to make lighter . . . While 'tis day.

In the fields of the Master gleaning . . . May my hands and heart be strong . . . May I know life's deepest meaning . . . May I sing life's sweetest song . . . With some faithful friends to love me . . . May I always do my best . . . And at last with heaven above me . . . Let me rest.

(From an old reward of merit card)

Oh, the blessing it is to have a friend to whom we can speak fearlessly on any subject; one with whom one's deepest as well as one's most foolish thoughts come out simply and safely. Oh, the comfort, the inexpressible comfort of feeling safe with a person, having neither to weigh thoughts nor measure words, but pouring them all right out just as they come, chaff and grain together, certain that a faithful hand will take and sift them, keep what is worth keeping and then, with breath of kindness, blow the rest away. Author Unknown

I'd rather see a sermon . . . Than to hear one any day . . . I'd rather one should walk with me . . . Than merely show the way . . . The eye's a better pupil . . . And more willing than the ear . . . Fine counsel is confusing . . . But example's always clear . . . And best of all the preachers . . . Are the men who live their creeds . . . For to see good. put in action . . . Is what everybody needs.

I soon can learn to do it . . . If you'll let me see it done . . . I can see your hands in action . . . But your tongue too fast may run . . . And the lecture you deliver . . . May be very fine and true . . . But I'd rather get my lesson . . . By observing what you do . . . For I may misunderstand you . . . And the high advice you give . . . But there's no misunderstanding . . . How you act and how you live! Edgar A. Guest ©

Our minutes are like precious gold . . . To save or throw away . . . They either bring us joy untold . . . Or sorrow and dismay . . . So give to every day its due . . . In honest, earnest toil . . . The harvest pays in measure true . . . As each man tills his soil . . . 'Tis he, who ever daily spends . . . His time in useful ways . . . Who reaps rich store of dividends . . . In happy future days. Author Unknown

Oh, it's just the little homely things . . . The unobtrusive friendly things . . . The "Won't-you-let-me-help-you" things . . . That make our pathway light . . . The "Laugh-with-me-it's-funny" things . . . And it's the jolly, joking things . . . The "Never-mind-the-trouble" things . . . That make the world seem bright . . . For all the countless famous things . . . The wondrous record-breaking things . . . These "Never-can-be-equalled" things . . . That all the papers cite . . . Are not the little human things . . . The "Everyday-encountered" things . . . The "Just-because-I-like-you" things . . . That make us happy quite . . . So here's to all the little things . . . The "Done-and-then-forgotten" things . . . Those "Oh-it's-simply-nothing" things . . . That make life worth the fight.

Author Unknown

❋

Should you feel inclined to censure . . . Faults you may in others view . . . Ask your own heart, ere you venture . . . If that has not failings, too . . . Let not friendly vows be broken . . . Rather strive a friend to gain . . . Many a word in anger spoken . . . Finds its passage home again . . . Do not, then, in idle pleasure . . . Trifle with a brother's fame . . . Guard it as a valued treasure . . . Sacred as your own good name . . . Do not form opinions blindly . . . Hastiness to trouble tends . . . Those of whom we thought unkindly . . . Oft become our warmest friends.

Author Unknown

❋

Happy is he who has learned the way . . . To live with others day by day . . . Whose disposition constantly . . . Reflects a mind that e'er is freed . . . From pettiness of thought and deed.

Happy is he who does not frown . . . At little things that get him down . . . Who laughs it off and goes his way . . . Not spoiling other people's day . . . With bitter things he has to say.

Happy is he who has such grace . . . That criticism he can face . . . Who boasteth not his own great deeds . . . But to suggestion always heeds . . . And sees the flowers not the weeds.

Happy is he whose own business he minds . . . Nor dwells on other's faults he finds . . . But with his own he does his best . . . And helps where'er he can the rest . . . This man, I think, is truly blest.

Hilda McGuire ©

❋

We are only certain of today . . . yesterday is gone and to-morrow is always coming.

Martin Vanbee

❋

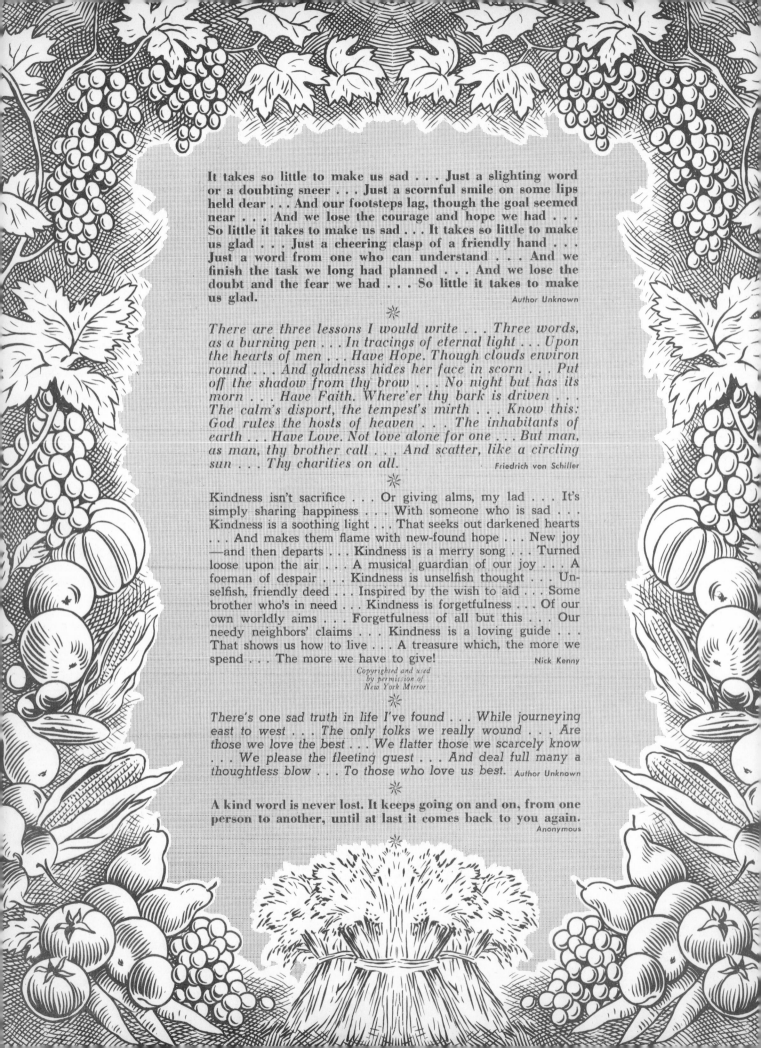

It takes so little to make us sad . . . Just a slighting word or a doubting sneer . . . Just a scornful smile on some lips held dear . . . And our footsteps lag, though the goal seemed near . . . And we lose the courage and hope we had . . . So little it takes to make us sad . . . It takes so little to make us glad . . . Just a cheering clasp of a friendly hand . . . Just a word from one who can understand . . . And we finish the task we long had planned . . . And we lose the doubt and the fear we had . . . So little it takes to make us glad.

Author Unknown

There are three lessons I would write . . . Three words, as a burning pen . . . In tracings of eternal light . . . Upon the hearts of men . . . Have Hope. Though clouds environ round . . . And gladness hides her face in scorn . . . Put off the shadow from thy brow . . . No night but has its morn . . . Have Faith. Where'er thy bark is driven . . . The calm's disport, the tempest's mirth . . . Know this: God rules the hosts of heaven . . . The inhabitants of earth . . . Have Love. Not love alone for one . . . But man, as man, thy brother call . . . And scatter, like a circling sun . . . Thy charities on all.

Friedrich von Schiller

Kindness isn't sacrifice . . . Or giving alms, my lad . . . It's simply sharing happiness . . . With someone who is sad . . . Kindness is a soothing light . . . That seeks out darkened hearts . . . And makes them flame with new-found hope . . . New joy —and then departs . . . Kindness is a merry song . . . Turned loose upon the air . . . A musical guardian of our joy . . . A foeman of despair . . . Kindness is unselfish thought . . . Unselfish, friendly deed . . . Inspired by the wish to aid . . . Some brother who's in need . . . Kindness is forgetfulness . . . Of our own worldly aims . . . Forgetfulness of all but this . . . Our needy neighbors' claims . . . Kindness is a loving guide . . . That shows us how to live . . . A treasure which, the more we spend . . . The more we have to give!

Nick Kenny

*Copyrighted and used
by permission of
New York Mirror*

There's one sad truth in life I've found . . . While journeying east to west . . . The only folks we really wound . . . Are those we love the best . . . We flatter those we scarcely know . . . We please the fleeting guest . . . And deal full many a thoughtless blow . . . To those who love us best. Author Unknown

A kind word is never lost. It keeps going on and on, from one person to another, until at last it comes back to you again.

Anonymous

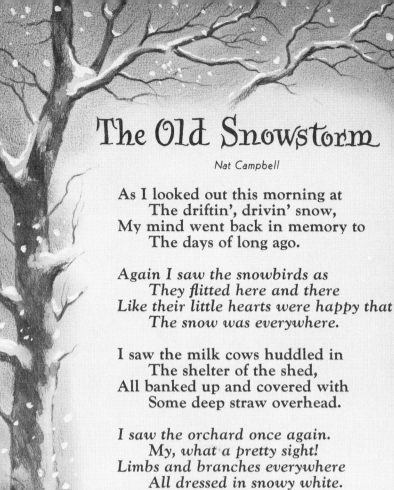

The Old Snowstorm

Nat Campbell

As I looked out this morning at
    The driftin', drivin' snow,
My mind went back in memory to
    The days of long ago.

Again I saw the snowbirds as
    They flitted here and there
Like their little hearts were happy that
    The snow was everywhere.

I saw the milk cows huddled in
    The shelter of the shed,
All banked up and covered with
    Some deep straw overhead.

I saw the orchard once again.
    My, what a pretty sight!
Limbs and branches everywhere
    All dressed in snowy white.

I saw the old creek runnin' there
    All frozen 'long its edge;
Saw th' white snow drifted 'long
    The old row of hedge.

Yes, an' 'long the old hedge-row,
    An' near the old hayracks,
In memory I really saw
    A lotta rabbit tracks.

I saw my older brother Jim
    Out there in th' shed
With th' hammer and a lotta nails
    A-fixin' up the sled.

I saw the meadow over there,
    All shining, pure and bright;
I don't believe I ever saw
    A thing on earth so white.

So, as for fetchin' memories
    There's nothin' that I know
That'll bring 'em back prettier than
    A real old-fashioned snow.

Acres of Diamonds

Russell H. Conwell
(1843-1925)

When going down the Tigris and Euphrates rivers many years ago with a party of English travelers, I found myself under the direction of an old Arab guide whom we hired up at Bagdad, and I have often thought how that guide resembled our barbers in certain mental characteristics. He thought that it was not only his duty to guide us down those rivers, and do what he was paid for doing, but also to entertain us with stories curious and weird, ancient and modern, strange and familiar. Many of them I have forgotten, and I am glad I have, but there is one I shall never forget . . .

The old guide told me that there once lived not far from the River Indus an ancient Persian by the name of Ali Hafed. He said that Ali Hafed owned a very large farm, that he had orchards, grain fields, and gardens; that he had money at interest, and was a wealthy and contented man. He was contented because he was wealthy, and wealthy because he was contented.

One day there visited that old Persian farmer one of those ancient Buddhist priests, one of the wise men of the East. He sat down by the fire and told the old farmer how this world of ours was made. He said that this world was once a mere bank of fog, and that the Almighty thrust His finger into this bank of fog, and began slowly to move His finger around, increasing the speed until at last He whirled this bank of fog into a solid ball of fire.

Then it went rolling through the universe, burning its way through other banks of fog, and condensed the moisture without, until it fell in floods of rain upon its hot surface, and cooled the outward crust. Then the internal fires bursting outward through the crust threw up the mountains and hills, the valleys, the plains and prairies of this wonderful world of ours. If this internal molten mass came bursting out and cooled very quickly it became granite; less quickly, copper; less quickly, silver; less quickly, gold; and, after gold, diamonds were made.

Said the old priest, "A diamond is a congealed drop of sunlight." Now that is literally scientifically true, that a diamond is an actual deposit of carbon from the sun. The old priest told Ali Hafed that if he had one diamond the size of his thumb he could purchase the county, and if he had a mine of diamonds he could place his children upon thrones through the influence of their great wealth.

Painting Opposite
GATHERING WOOD
George Henry Durrie
(1820-1863)
Museum of Fine Arts, Boston
The Karolik Collection

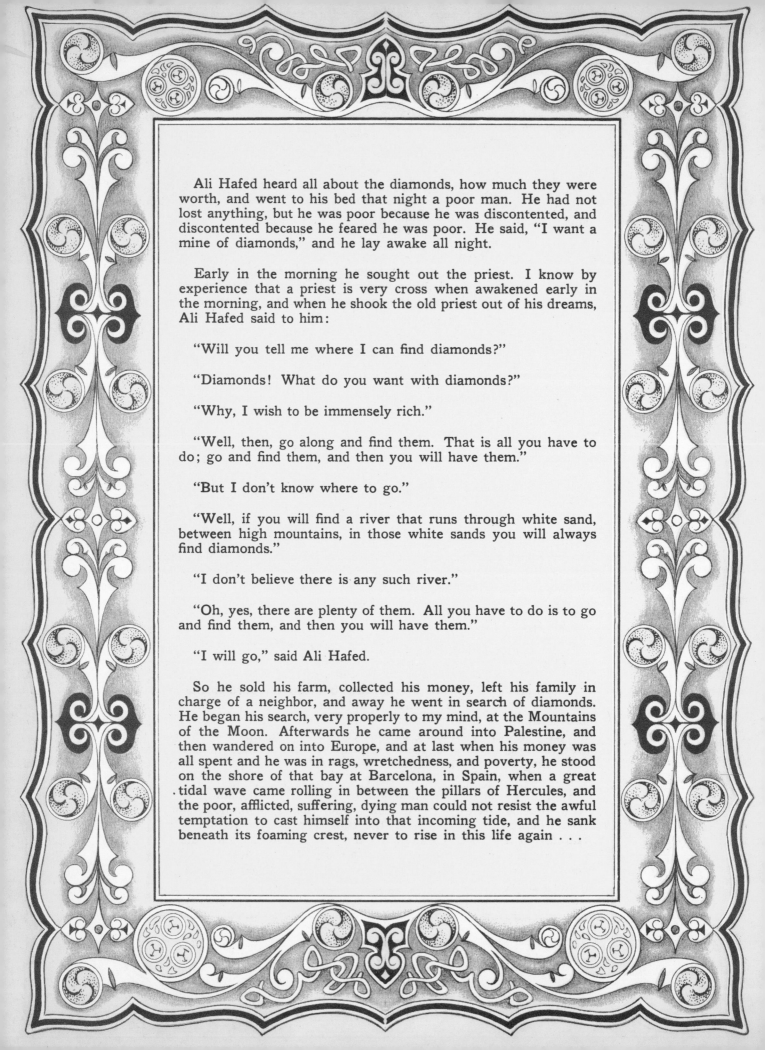

Ali Hafed heard all about the diamonds, how much they were worth, and went to his bed that night a poor man. He had not lost anything, but he was poor because he was discontented, and discontented because he feared he was poor. He said, "I want a mine of diamonds," and he lay awake all night.

Early in the morning he sought out the priest. I know by experience that a priest is very cross when awakened early in the morning, and when he shook the old priest out of his dreams, Ali Hafed said to him:

"Will you tell me where I can find diamonds?"

"Diamonds! What do you want with diamonds?"

"Why, I wish to be immensely rich."

"Well, then, go along and find them. That is all you have to do; go and find them, and then you will have them."

"But I don't know where to go."

"Well, if you will find a river that runs through white sand, between high mountains, in those white sands you will always find diamonds."

"I don't believe there is any such river."

"Oh, yes, there are plenty of them. All you have to do is to go and find them, and then you will have them."

"I will go," said Ali Hafed.

So he sold his farm, collected his money, left his family in charge of a neighbor, and away he went in search of diamonds. He began his search, very properly to my mind, at the Mountains of the Moon. Afterwards he came around into Palestine, and then wandered on into Europe, and at last when his money was all spent and he was in rags, wretchedness, and poverty, he stood on the shore of that bay at Barcelona, in Spain, when a great tidal wave came rolling in between the pillars of Hercules, and the poor, afflicted, suffering, dying man could not resist the awful temptation to cast himself into that incoming tide, and he sank beneath its foaming crest, never to rise in this life again . . .

The man who purchased Ali Hafed's farm one day led his camel into the garden to drink, and as that camel put its nose into the shallow water of that garden brook, Ali Hafed's successor noticed a curious flash of light from the white sands of the stream. He pulled out a black stone having an eye of light reflecting all the hues of the rainbow. He took the pebble into the house and put it on the mantel which covers the central fires, and forgot all about it.

A few days later this same old priest came in to visit Ali Hafed's successor, and the moment he opened that drawing-room door he saw that flash of light on the mantel, and rushed up to it, and shouted: "Here is a diamond! Has Ali Hafed returned?" "Oh, no, Ali Hafed has not returned, and this is not a diamond. It is nothing but a stone we found right out here in our own garden." "But," said the priest, "I tell you I know a diamond when I see it. I know positively that is a diamond."

Then together they rushed out into that old garden and stirred up the white sands with their fingers, and lo! there came up other more beautiful and valuable gems than the first. "Thus," said the guide to me, and, friends, it is historically true, "was discovered the diamond mine of Golconda, the most magnificent diamond mine in all the history of mankind, excelling the Kimberley itself. The Kohinoor, and the Orloff of the crown jewels of England and Russia, the largest on earth, came from that mine."

When that old Arab guide told me the second chapter of his story, he then took off his Turkish cap and swung it around in the air again to get my attention to the moral. Those Arab guides have morals to their stories. As he swung his hat, he said to me, "Had Ali Hafed remained at home and dug in his own cellar, or underneath his own wheatfields, or in his own garden, instead of wretchedness, starvation, and death by suicide in a strange land, he would have had acres of diamonds. For every acre of that old farm, yes, every shovelful, afterwards revealed gems which since have decorated the crowns of monarchs."

When he added the moral to his story I saw why he had reserved it for "his special friends". But I did not tell him I could see it. It was that mean old Arab's way of going around a thing like a lawyer, to say indirectly what he did not dare say directly, that "in his private opinion there was a certain young man then traveling down the Tigris River that might better be at home in America".

Featured through the courtesy
of Harper & Brothers, Publishers.